LIBRA
WITCH
♎

© JAMES C. WELCH

Ivo Dominguez, Jr. (Georgetown, DE) has been active in the magickal community since 1978. He is one of the founders of Keepers of the Holly Chalice, the first Assembly of the Sacred Wheel coven. He currently serves as one of the Elders in the Assembly. Ivo is the author of several books, including *The Four Elements of the Wise* and *Practical Astrology for Witches and Pagans*. In his mundane life, he has been a computer programmer, the executive director of an AIDS/HIV service organization, a bookstore owner, and many other things. Visit him at www.ivodominguezjr.com.

About the Authors

©AARON WERNER

Patti Wigington has been a Pagan and witch since 1987. In addition to a full-time job in the corporate world, Patti was editor of the Paganism & Wicca site at LearnReligions, previously About.com, from 2007 to 2020. She is a priestess, a blogger, and the author of several books, including *Daily Spell Journal*, *Witchcraft for Healing*, *Badass Ancestors*, and *The Witch's Complete Guide to Tarot*. Patti has a BA in History from Ohio University and a graduate certificate in Management & Leadership, and she lives in a magical cottage in the woods of Southeastern Ohio. For more on Patti's work, please visit www.pattiwigington.com.

• UNLOCK THE MAGIC OF YOUR SUN SIGN •

LIBRA
WITCH

♎

IVO DOMINGUEZ, JR.
PATTI WIGINGTON

Llewellyn Publications
Woodbury, Minnesota

FIRST EDITION
First Printing, 2024

Art direction and cover design by Shira Atakpu
Book design by Christine Ha
Interior art by the Llewellyn Art Department
Tarot Original 1909 Deck © 2021 with art created by Pamela Colman Smith and Arthur Edward Waite. Used with permission of LoScarabeo.
The Libra Correspondences appendix is excerpted with permission from *Llewellyn's Complete Book of Correspondences: A Comprehensive & Cross-Referenced Resource for Pagans & Wiccans* © 2013 by Sandra Kynes.

Llewellyn Publications is a registered trademark of Llewellyn Worldwide Ltd.

Library of Congress Cataloging-in-Publication Data (Pending)
ISBN: 978-0-7387-7286-8

Llewellyn Worldwide Ltd. does not participate in, endorse, or have any authority or responsibility concerning private business transactions between our authors and the public.

All mail addressed to the author is forwarded but the publisher cannot, unless specifically instructed by the author, give out an address or phone number.

Any internet references contained in this work are current at publication time, but the publisher cannot guarantee that a specific location will continue to be maintained. Please refer to the publisher's website for links to authors' websites and other sources.

Llewellyn Publications
A Division of Llewellyn Worldwide Ltd.
2143 Wooddale Drive
Woodbury, MN 55125-2989
www.llewellyn.com
Printed in the United States of America

Other Books by Ivo Dominguez, Jr.

The Four Elements of the Wise
Keys to Perception: A Practical Guide to Psychic Development
Practical Astrology for Witches and Pagans
Casting Sacred Space
Spirit Speak

Other Books by Patti Wigington

Badass Ancestors

Other Books in The Witch's Sun Sign Series

Aries Witch
Taurus Witch
Gemini Witch
Cancer Witch
Leo Witch
Virgo Witch
Scorpio Witch
Sagittarius Witch
Capricorn Witch
Aquarius Witch
Pisces Witch

CONTENTS

✳ Contents ✳

SPELLS, RECIPES, AND PRACTICES

INTRODUCTION

Ivo Dominguez, Jr.

This is the seventh book in the Witch's Sun Sign series. There are twelve volumes in this series with a book for every Sun sign, but with a special focus on witchcraft. This series explores and honors the gifts, perspectives, and joys of being a witch through the perspective of their Sun sign. Each book has information on how your sign affects your magick and life experiences with insights provided by witches of your Sun sign, as well as spells, rituals, and practices to enrich your witchcraft. This series is geared toward helping witches grow, develop, and integrate the power of their Sun sign into all their practices. Each book in the series has ten writers, so there are many takes on the meaning of being a witch of a particular sign. All the books in the Witch's Sun Sign series are a sampler of possibilities, with pieces that are deep, fun, practical, healing, instructive, revealing, and authentic.

Welcome to the Libra Witch

I'm Ivo Dominguez, Jr., and I've been a witch and an astrologer for over forty years. In this book, and in the whole series, I've written the chapters focused on astrological information and collaborated with the other writers. For the sake of transparency, I am a Sagittarius, and most of the nine other writers for this book are Libras.[1] The chapters focused on the lived experience of being a Libra witch were written by my coauthor, Patti Wigington, who has been a Pagan and witch since 1987 and is the founder and high priestess of a coven. She is an author whose works include *Witchcraft for Healing*, *Badass Ancestors*, and *The Witch's Complete Guide to Tarot*. The spells and shorter pieces written for this book come from a diverse group of strong Libra witches. Their practices will give you a deeper understanding of yourself as a Libra and as a witch. With the information, insights, and methods offered here, your Libra nature and your witchcraft will be better united. The work of becoming fully yourself entails finding, refining, and merging all the parts that make up your life and identity. This all sounds very serious, but the content of this book will run from lighthearted to profound to do justice to the topic. Moreover, this book has practical suggestions on using the power of your Sun sign to improve your craft as a

---

1. The exceptions are Dawn Aurora Hunt, who contributes a recipe for each sign in the series, and Sandra Kynes, whose correspondences are listed in the appendix. They are Scorpios.

witch. There are many books on Libra or astrology or witch-craft; this book is about wholeheartedly being a Libra witch.

There is a vast amount of material available in books, blogs, memes, and videos targeted at Libra. The content presented in these ranges from serious to snarky, and a fair amount of it is less than accurate or useful. After reading this book, you will be better equipped to tell which of these you can take to heart and use, and which are fine for a laugh but not much more. There is a good chance you will be flipping back to reread some chapters to get a better understanding of some of the points being made. This book is meant to be read more than once, and some parts of it may become reference material you will use for years. Consider keeping a folder, digital or paper, for your notes and ideas on being a Libra witch.

What You Will Need

Knowing your Sun sign is enough to get quite a bit out of this book. However, to use all the material in this book, you will need your birth chart to verify your Moon sign and rising sign. In addition to your birth date, you will need the location and the time of your birth as exactly as possible. If you don't know your birth time, try to get a copy of your birth certificate (though not all birth certificates list times). If it is reasonable and you feel comfortable, you can ask family members for information. They may remember an exact time, but even narrowing it down to a range of hours will be useful. There is a solution to not having your exact birth time. Since it takes moments to create birth charts using software, you can run birth charts that are thirty minutes apart over the span of hours that contains your possible birth times. By reading the chapters that describe the characteristics of Moon signs and rising signs, you can reduce the pile of possible charts to a few contenders. Read the descriptions and find the chart whose combination of Moon sign and rising sign rings true to you. There are more refined techniques a professional astrologer can use to get closer to a chart that is more accurate. However, knowing your Sun sign, Moon sign, and rising sign is all you need for this book. There are numerous websites that offer free basic birth charts you can view online. For a fee, more detailed charts are available on these sites.

You may want to have an astrological wall calendar or an astrological day planner to keep track of the sign and phase of the Moon. You will want to keep track of what your ruling planet, Venus, is doing. Over time as your knowledge grows, you'll probably start looking at where all the planets are, what aspects they are making, and when they are retrograde or direct. You could do this all on an app or a website, but it is often easier to flip through a calendar or planner to see what is going on. Flipping forward and back through the weeks and months ahead can give you a better sense of how to prepare for upcoming celestial influences. Moreover, the calendars and planners contain basic background information about astrology and are a great start for studying astrology.

You're a Libra and So Much More

Every person is unique, complex, and a mixture of traits that can clash, complement, compete, or collaborate with each other. This book focuses on your Libra Sun sign and provides starting points for understanding your Moon sign and rising sign. It cannot answer all your questions or be a perfect fit because of all the other parts that make you an individual. However, you will find more than enough to enrich and deepen your witchcraft as a Libra. There will also be descriptions you won't agree with or you think do not portray you. In some instances, you will be correct, and in other cases, you may come around to acknowledging that the information does apply to you. Astrology can be used for magick, divination, personal development, and more. No matter the purpose, your understanding of astrology will change over time as your life unfolds and your experience and self-knowledge broaden. You will probably return to this book several times as you find opportunities to use more of the insights and methods.

This may seem like strange advice to find in a book for the Libra witch, but remember that you are more than a Libra witch. In the process of claiming the identity of being a witch, it is common to want to have a clear and firm definition of who you are. Sometimes this means overidentifying with a category, such as fire witch, herb witch, crystal witch, kitchen witch, and so on. It is useful to become aware of the affinities you have so long as you do not limit and bind yourself to being less than you are. The best use for this book is to uncover all the Libra parts of you so you can integrate them well. The finest witches I know have well-developed specialties but also are well rounded in their knowledge and practices.

Onward!

With all that said, the Sun is the starting point for your power and your journey as a witch. The first chapter is about the profound influence your Sun sign has, so don't skip through the table of contents; please start at the beginning. After that, Patti will dive into magick and practices that come naturally to Libra witches. I'll be walking you through the benefits of picking the right times, places, and things to energize your Libra magick. Patti will also share a couple of real-life personal stories on how to manage the busy lives that Libras choose, as well as advice on the best ways to protect yourself spiritually and set good boundaries when you really need to. I'll introduce you to how your Moon sign and your rising sign shape your witchcraft. Patti offers great stories about how her Libra nature comes forward in her life as a witch, and then gives suggestions on self-care and self-awareness. I'll share a full ritual with you to call on the spirit of your sign. Lastly, Patti offers her wisdom on how to become a better Libra witch. Throughout the whole book, you'll find tables of correspondences, spells, recipes, practices, and other treasures to add to your practices.

HOW YOUR SUN POWERS YOUR MAGICK

Ivo Dominguez, Jr.

The first bit of astrology people generally learn is their Sun sign. Some enthusiastically embrace the meaning of their Sun sign and apply it to everything in their life. They feel their Sun is shining and all is well in the world. Then at some point, they'll encounter someone who will, with a bit of disdain, enlighten them on the limits of Sun sign astrology. They feel their Sun isn't enough, and they scramble to catch up. What comes next is usually the discovery that they have a Moon sign, a rising sign, and all the rest of the planets in an assortment of signs. Making sense of all this additional information is daunting as it requires quite a bit of learning and/or an astrologer to guide you through the process. Wherever you are on this journey into the world of astrology, at some point you will circle back around and rediscover that the Sun is still in the center.

The Sun in your birth chart shows where life and spirit came into the world to form you. It is the keeper of your spark of spirit and the wellspring of your power. Your Sun is in Libra, so that is the flavor, the color, the type of energy that is at your core. You are your whole birth chart, but it is your Libra Sun that provides the vital force that moves throughout all parts of your life. When you work in harmony and alignment with your Sun, you have access to more life and the capacity to live it better. This is true for all people, but this advice takes on a special meaning for those who are witches. The root of a witch's magick power is revealed by their Sun sign. You can draw on many kinds of energy, but the type of energy you attract with greatest ease is Libra. The more awareness and intention you apply to connecting with and acting as a conduit for that Libra Sun, the more effective you will be as a witch.

The more you learn about the meaning of a Libra Sun, the easier it will be to find ways to make that connection. To be effective in magick, divination, and other categories of workings, it is vital to understand yourself—your motivations, drives, attractions, etc.—so you can refine your intentions, questions, and desired outcomes. Understanding your Sun sign is an important step in that process. One of the goals shared by both witchcraft and astrology is to affirm and to integrate the totality of your nature to live your best life. The glyph for the Sun in astrology is a dot with a circle

around it. Your Libra Sun is the dot and the circle, your center, and your circumference. It is your
beginning and your journey. It is also the core of
your personal Wheel of the Year, the seasons of your life that
repeat, have resonances, but are never the same.

How Libra Are You?

The Sun is the hub around which the planets circle. Its gravity pulls the planets to keep them in their courses and bends
space-time to create the place we call our solar system. The
Sun in your birth chart tugs on every other part of your
chart in a similar way. Everything is both bound and free,
affected but seeking its own direction. When people encounter descriptions of Libra traits, they will often begin to make
a list of which things apply to them and which don't. Some
will say they are the epitome of Libra traits, others will claim
that they are barely Libra, and many will be somewhere in
between. Evaluating how closely or not you align with the
traditional characteristics of a Libra is a particularly useful
approach to understanding your sign. If you are a Libra, you
have all the Libra traits somewhere within you. What varies
from person to person is the expression of those traits. Some
traits express fully in a classic form, others are blocked from
expressing or are modified, and sometimes there is a reaction
to behave as the opposite of what is expected. As a Libra,
and especially as a witch, you have the capacity to activate

dormant traits, to shape functioning traits, and to tone down overactive traits.

The characteristics and traits of signs are tendencies, drives, and affinities. Gravity encourages a ball to roll down a hill. A plant's leaves will grow in the direction of sunlight. The warmth of a fire will draw people together on a cold night. A flavor you enjoy will entice you to take another bite of your food. Your Libra Sun urges you to be and to act like a Libra. That said, you also have free will and volition to make other choices. Moreover, the rest of your birth chart and the ever-changing celestial influences are also shaping your options, moods, and drives. The more you become aware of the traits and behaviors that come with being a Libra, the easier it will be to choose how you express them. Most people want to have the freedom to make their own choices, but for a Libra, it is essential.

As a witch, you have additional tools to work with the Libra energy. You can choose when to access and how you shape the qualities of Libra as they come forth in your life. You can summon the energy of Libra, name the traits you desire, and manifest them. You can also banish or neutralize or ground what you don't need. You can find where your Libra energy short-circuits, where it glitches, and unblock it. You can examine your uncomfortable feelings and your less-than-perfect behaviors to seek the shadowed places within so you can heal or integrate them. Libra is also a spirit and a current of collective consciousness that is vast in size—a group mind and archetype. Libra is not limited to humanity; it engages with plants, animals, minerals, and all the physical and nonphysical beings of the Earth and all its associated realms. As a witch, you can call upon and work with the spiritual entity that is Libra. You can live your life as a ritual. The motion of your life can be a dance to the tune and rhythm of the heavens.

The Libra Glyph

The simplest interpretation for Libra's glyph is that it represents the scales that are the emblem for the sign. The parallel lines with a partial circle in the center of the upper line can also be seen as the Sun  on the horizon. Libra is the sign that is dusk to Aries' dawn, the autumn in the northern hemisphere, and marks the descendant. The glyph can also be seen as two parallel lines with the Greek letter omega superimposed on the upper line. Omega is the last letter and represents the end, resolution, or completion of things. Libra's search for ultimate meanings and purposes is encoded in the glyph. The parallel lines are horizontal; all the air sign glyphs contain horizontal lines because the winds circle the Earth, touching everything. They carry sounds, humidity, scents, and spiritual influences to every place and person. In the pictographic code of the astrological glyphs, circles represent spirit and semicircles represent soul. Spirit is the part of you that is eternal, and soul is the part that is shaped and changed by the experiences of incarnation. The semicircle at the top of the glyph shows that Libras need to infuse soul and spirit into all they do.

Use your imagination to see this glyph as a representation of how you have a relationship with all you observe. The symmetry of the glyph also suggests the capacity to find harmony between all things. As the scales, it reminds you that you are the one who adds or subtracts from the pans to bring balance. As the setting Sun, the glyph reminds you to be present in your life. As an expanded omega, the glyph asks you to look to your directions and intentions.

By meditating on the glyph, you will develop a deeper understanding of what it is to be a Libra. You may also come up with your own personal gnosis or story about the glyph that can be a key that is uniquely yours. The glyph for Libra can be used in a similar fashion to the scribing of an invoking pentacle that is used to open the gates to the elemental realms. However, instead of the elemental realms, this glyph opens the way to the realm of mind and spirit that is the source of Libra. To make this glyph work, you need to deeply ingrain the feeling of scribing this glyph. Visually, it is a simple glyph, so memorizing it is easy, but having a kinesthetic feel for it turns it into magick. Spend some time doodling the glyph on paper. Try drawing the glyph on your palm with a finger for several repetitions as that adds several layers of sensation and memory patterns.

Whenever you need access to more of your magickal energy, scribe the Libra glyph in your mind, on your hand, in the air—however you can. Then pull and channel and feel your center fill with whatever you need. It takes very little time to open this connection using the glyph. Consider making this one of the practices you use to get ready to do divination, spell work, ritual, or just to start your day.

Libra Patterns

This is a short list of patterns, guidelines, and predilections for Libra Sun people to get you started. If you keep a book of shadows, or a journal, or files on a digital device to record your thoughts and insights on magickal work, you may wish to create your own list to expand upon these. The process of observing, summarizing, and writing down your own ideas in a list is a great way to learn about your sign.

- Whether in the background or on the forefront of their mind, Libra is always aware of relationships and connections. These can be between people, colors, sounds, concepts, philosophies, and so on. This is the Libran way of understanding the world.

- Like the scales that are the sign's emblem, Libras care more about finding balance than what is in the scale's pans. Fairness, impartiality, and equanimity are important Libran values.

(◎) Because you perceive so many angles and sides to every question and situation, you use a considerable amount of time and energy in perceiving, thinking, and contemplating before you act. You work so hard in this process that sometimes you feel tired enough to fool yourself into thinking that you're done before you've acted.

(◎) One of the Libran spiritual quests is to go beyond mere balance to find reconciliation, harmony, and synthesis. Resolving polarities is a big part of your spiritual work.

(◎) Libra is opposite to Aries on the wheel and is the seventh sign in the journey of the zodiac. While Aries has a great focus on themselves as an individual, Libra concentrates on what it means to be part of a we or an us while still maintaining selfhood.

(◎) All one-on-one relationships, whether these be friends, lovers, coworkers, or enemies, loom large in your inner life. With Venus as your ruling planet, you are more emotional than the other air signs.

(◎) Truth, or as close to truth as human perception allows, is a touchstone for Libra. Equally important is compassion; remember that Venus rules Libra. Most Libras are challenged regularly by circumstances where it appears that the choice is between telling the truth and offering kindness.

(◎) Your attention is drawn to the extremes and edges of life such as peace and war, the primal and the civilized, frivolity and profundity, and to all colors and contrasts that bring life into high relief. Although your tendency is to bring these into balance or average them into the middle path, allow yourself to experience the extremes so that you truly understand them.

(◎) Happiness and success are more easily realized when you decide you've heard and thought enough; you make up your mind and implement your choice. You can't please everyone, so choose and move on. You will have more opportunities and options to adjust your course if you use up less time pondering.

A Libra Sun comes with a desire to be liked by as many people as possible. However, you also want to find the right balance between your needs and the needs of others. You also want to live authentically and avoid conflict with others. Ultimately, the most significant balance and relationship to maintain is between you and the person you see in the mirror.

Despite a reputation of wanted peace and concord, Libras are pulled toward contradictions, paradoxes, inconsistencies, the one note that is off in a chord, and so on. This is because the snag, the outlier, the rough spot that needs smoothing, provides an interesting task that promises the reward of creating order and harmony.

Normally your capacity for dialogue and sociability serves you and others well. When you are stressed or uncomfortable, you may share too much information and cross the line into gossip. Another symptom that you've exceeded your coping skills is indulging in sweet or fatty foods.

◎) Libras are adept at using manners, social expectations, and conventions as tools for reducing conflict and managing expectations. Most are also good at code-switching to match the culture and norms of different groups of people in different settings.

◎) Like all air signs, you need regular mental stimulation, but in your case, it must relate to one of your standing interests. This could be the arts, nature, the study of people, causes, and so on, because for you, even pleasure must have broader meanings.

◎) Learn to love physical activity, whether it be dance, walking, sports, Pilates, and so on. Your body needs to balance all that mental activity with physical exertion.

◎) Since your personal development style is often connected to other people, there is a risk of becoming dependent on others. Don't become *the giving tree* (look this up online if you aren't familiar) and sing your own praises as often as you praise others.

Cardinal Air

The four elements come in sets of three that repeat. The modalities known as cardinal, fixed, and mutable are three different flavors or styles of manifestation for the elements. The twelvefold pattern that is the backbone of astrology comes from the twelve combinations produced from four elements times  three modalities. As you go around the wheel of the zodiac, the order of the elements is always fire, earth, air, then water, while the modalities are always in the order of cardinal, fixed, then mutable. Each season begins in the cardinal modality, reaches its peak in the fixed modality, and transforms to the next season in the mutable modality. The cardinal modality is the energy of creation bursting forth, coming into being, and spreading throughout the world. The fixed modality is the harmonization of energy so that it becomes and remains fully itself and is preserved. Fixed does not mean static or passive; it is the work of maintaining creation. The mutable modality is the energy of flux that is flexibility, transformation, death, and rebirth.

Libra is the seventh sign in the zodiac, so it is air of the cardinal modality. This is why a Libra witch can call upon deep reserves of mental energy and the ability to find meaningful connections. Although as a Libra witch you can call upon air in all its forms, it is easiest to draw upon cardinal air.

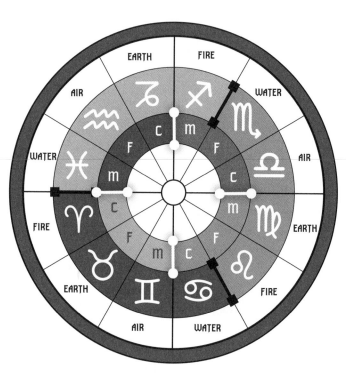

The elements and modalities on the wheel

Venus, Your Ruling Planet

Your Sun sign determines the source and the type of energy you have in your core. The ruling planet for a sign reveals your go-to moves and your intuitive or habitual responses for expressing that energy. Your ruling planet provides a curated set of prebuilt responses and custom-tailored stances for you to use in day-to-day life. Venus is the ruling planet for Libra. The first association that springs to mind for many on hearing the name Venus is the Roman goddess of love. However, the planet Venus and how it influences Libra is more complicated, and the amorous qualities are just a fraction of what it brings. Venus is beauty in all its forms and is the capacity to perceive beauty. The emphasis on beauty is intertwined with and arises from Venus's focus on harmony, balance, and justice. The influence of Venus is modified by the air of Libra to focus more on ideas about beauty, philosophies of aesthetics, and more refined expressions of this planet's powers.

Libra witches are more strongly affected by whatever Venus is doing in the heavens. It is useful to keep track of the aspects that Venus is making with other planets. You can get basic information on what aspects mean and when they are happening in astrological calendars and online resources. You will feel Venus retrogrades more strongly than most people, but you can find ways to make them useful periods to analyze what you've already done. Libra witches will notice that the impact of the Venus retrograde will start earlier and end a few days later than the listed duration. Also, when Venus in the heavens is in Libra, you will feel an extra boost of energy. The first step to using the power of Venus is to pay attention to what it is doing, how you feel, and what is happening in your life.

Witches have the gift to shift their relationship with the powers they work with and the powers that influence them. As a Libra witch, you are connected to the power of Venus. By paying close attention to how those energies affect you, it becomes possible to harness those energies to purposes you choose. Venus can be as great a source of energy for a Libra witch as the element of air. Although there is some overlap between the qualities and capacities assigned to Venus and air, the differences are greater. Venus shapes how you feel about and perceive the world around you. Air provides the words, concept, and process that allows you to examine your experiences and discuss them. Venus has the power to motivate or block your actions and to separate or join heart and mind. Air connects the minds and spirits of all beings. Venus is the source of all emotional exchanges and interactions, and most thoughts are tinged with emotion. Air is the principle of agency, interconnectedness, and composure that is neutral to emotion but can convey it. Over time, you can map out the overlapping regions and the differences between Venus and air. Using both planetary and elemental resources can give you a much broader range and more finesse.

Libra and the Zodiacal Wheel

The order of the signs in the zodiac can also be seen as a creation story where the run of the elements repeats three times. Libra is in the second third of the zodiac, which is the second appearance of the four elements in the story of the universe. Having come into existence, the goal of the elements at this point is to become fully themselves. Libra remembers their purposes for coming into being. The air of Libra is dynamic and focused on unfolding the possibilities of existence in relationship to others. The air of Libra is the most refined of all the versions of the element of air.

Although true for all witches, the Libra witch needs to apply themselves to discovering who they are and what their role is in the physical and spiritual realms. When you can regularly connect with your role and relationships, you become a conduit for your magick, and the people and projects that matter to you will flourish. This is the full expression of being in the second quarter of the zodiac. You can make progress in this quest through meditation and inner journeys, but that alone will not do. The Libra witch learns by doing, seeing, touching, talking, thinking, taking measured actions, and repeating the process. Although Libras are sometimes stereotyped as being indecisive or too focused on seeking approval, it is more accurate to say that they are trying to create beauty and fairness in a world that is fraught with contradiction. When a Libra witch connects to the spiritual qualities of their air, they become an advocate and a voice for the magick of the world.

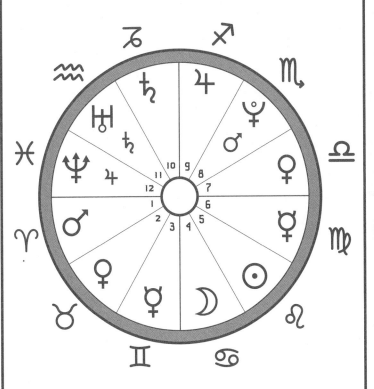

The sign and planet rulers on zodiac wheel

LIBRA
CORRESPONDENCES

♎

Power: To Balance

Keyword: Negotiation

Roles: Artist, Idealist, Arbiter

Ruling Planet: Venus ♀

Element: Cardinal Air

Colors: Pink, Lavender, and Light Blue

Shape: Heptagon

Metals: Copper

Body Part Ruled: Lower Back

Day of the Week: Friday

Affirmation:
When I work with what is given,
I create beauty and serenity.

WITCHCRAFT THAT COMES NATURALLY TO A LIBRA

Patti Wigington

S o, you're a Libra witch—you're an air sign, and by now you've probably figured out many of the traits that this entails. When it comes to your magic, it can be incredibly valuable to draw on the tendencies that make us Libra witches who we are. After all, Libras are all about harmony and balance, collaboration, and justice—why not take advantage of that in your rituals and spellcrafting?

Conversely, there are some areas where we Libras occasionally fall short; we often overthink and overanalyze, and we're not really good at conforming just for the sake of pleasing others. These attributes can—if we're not mindful of them—present their own unique set of challenges for the Libra witch.

There's a popular misconception that Libras are terrible decision-makers. Nothing could be farther from the truth—we're *good* at making decisions! However, because we're natural mediators, we sometimes take our sweet time to make a choice or pick a side, because we're willing to look at multiple perspectives in each case. A Libra might make a slow decision, but it will be an informed and wise one—and they'll be confident with their choice, standing by it even if others want to argue about it.

Ruled by Venus, Libras often second-guess our own gifts because we're so busy trying to weigh all our options and consider different points of view. Also, we have a habit of questioning whether we're *really* intuitive—because we like to be logical. After all, it's possible our intuition was right … but *maybe* it was just a lucky guess. It's the classic Libra dilemma. If you're a Libra, you're probably highly intuitive, so learning to trust your own perception and judgment will speed things along. Most Libras spend a lot of time reflecting on self-doubt when it comes to ourselves—and sometimes even going into utter denial about our own psychic abilities—but we're usually spot-on when we're considering other people. Chances are good that our premonitions, sense of déjà vu, or even abilities to recognize past lives are pretty accurate if we're looking at someone other than ourselves.

The Libra witch is well known for the gift of diplomacy, which makes them highly effective when it comes to spell work for peace, balance, and harmony. Need someone to resolve a conflict in your life? Find the nearest Libra witch, and they'll magically mediate the heck out of the situation—before you know it, everyone will be acting like old friends. Libra witches are great at spell work for beauty and happiness—and that includes glamour spells and illusions. We may not worry too much about how we look when we glance in the mirror, because we know that other people will see us the way we *want* them to view us.

When it comes to divination, again, the Libra witch excels at any practice that relies on intuition, such as tarot and scrying. Gifts of clairvoyance are typically a natural skill set for Libras, especially when it comes to matters of love, relationships, and harmonious connections. Libra witches are also highly skilled at visualization, due in no small part to their inherent creativity, a gift that comes in handy when manifesting our intentions into reality. Finally, Libras are often highly empathic. We're *very* good listeners, and people will tell us just about anything—fortunately, we also happen to be expert-level secret keepers. Libras often know what emotions other people are feeling whether they've articulated them to us verbally or not.

Deities, Spirits, and Archetypes for Libra Witches

Libra is the only zodiac sign that isn't depicted as a person or an animal—instead, we've got the scales and all they represent. Having a Sun sign associated with balance, truth, justice, and beauty lends itself well to working with a number of related deities, archetypes, and spirits.

In classical Greek mythology, Themis, the goddess of justice, joined her daughter Astraea in carrying the scales of justice. Libra witches can call upon these two powerful deities for workings related to fairness, balance, and harmony; if you've got a court case coming up, and you know you're in the right, consider petitioning Themis and Astraea for assistance. Libra is also deeply connected to Aphrodite, the goddess of love and beauty, a deity who can lend a hand in matters of relationships, romantic connections, and attraction. Hera, the Greek goddess of marriage—and wife of Zeus—has ties to the traits of the Libra witch as well. Despite her husband's repeated indiscretions, for which Hera exacted punishment upon Zeus's side partners, she chose to stay in the marriage. While Hera raged against Zeus's constant infidelity, she also weighed the benefits of maintaining the relationship.

The Norse goddess Freya is strongly related to the Libra spirit. Freya has a deep love for things of beauty and, like many Libras, finds a balance between passion and war. Associated with love, sex, and fertility, Freya also has powers of divine prophecy, and knows everything there is to know about magic and sorcery; she's said to embody the archetype of the *völva* (soothsayer), and brought her knowledge of magic to the gods.

The Sun god Shamash was associated in Mesopotamia with justice, fairness, and truth. He governed the entire universe, holding a staff and ring as symbols of righteousness, and he represents ethical, just behavior.

Ma'at, the Egyptian goddess of truth and divine order, was the wife of Thoth and daughter of Ra. She was revered in the Old Kingdom as a symbol of balance—something we Libras can certainly relate to. When someone died, their heart was weighed against a feather by Anubis; if they led a just and fair life, there would be balance between the two, and they were escorted to join with the divine for all eternity. Ma'at often serves as a reminder that although our natural inclination is to *fix* things, sometimes we can resolve issues simply by listening and being fair.

Among the Orishas of African traditional religions, Oshun is associated with love and relationships. She is a goddess of harmony and grace, related to Venus placement, and can be a powerful deity to work with in matters of interpersonal connections.

In tarot, the Libra sign is often represented by the Justice card, the eleventh card of the Major Arcana. Typically portrayed by a figure holding a pair of scales, this card epitomizes our quest for balance in all aspects of our lives—relationships, professional success, spiritual growth, and emotional stability. The classic Libra is not only intuitive, but they also dislike chaos and disorder—subsequently, they'll weigh their intuition with structure, reaching an outcome that satisfies the need for both. Libras are likeable truth-seekers…but they won't stand for anyone running rough-shod over them. The Justice card arms us with a sword to cut through obstacles that might be in our way.

Magical Practices for Libras

Most Libras are creative souls, due in no small part to our love of all things beautiful. If we can't find beauty in the world, we simply go ahead and create it ourselves. That's a valuable skill to draw upon when it comes to magic—when we don't see what we want, we visualize it into being, manifesting our deepest desires and goals.

Vision Boards

The vision board, which is a visual and tangible summary of your goals, is a magical practice that's a natural fit for the Libra witch—we're highly gifted in matters of setting our intention and then seeing it turn into reality. Many people believe that practices like visualization help us feel more motivated and confident, and thus more likely to take deliberate actions that make our dreams come true. Use your innate Libra love of aesthetics and order to craft a vision board that's uniquely yours, and you'll be manifesting your goals—magical or mundane—in no time.

Before you create a vision board of your own, it's important to reflect on what you hope to achieve—after all, you need a destination before you begin the journey. Consider what it is you wish to change in your life; do you want to find inspiration? Abundance? Wellness and healing? Whatever it is, be clear on your intention.

First, you'll need a background on which to build your project. I've found that the foam display boards sold at craft stores work well, but you can also use a piece of paper or cardboard. If you're short on space, you can even create your vision board inside the pages of your favorite journal. If you're someone who really doesn't love paper, go digital! Create your vision board virtually using Pinterest or use a graphic design app like Canva—you can even make a vision board to serve as your phone or laptop's wallpaper.

Next, you'll need images and words that represent your intention. For instance, to feel more confident at work, you might select words or phrases like *empowered* or *professional* and images reflecting your idea of what a successful career looks like. If you're planning to manifest abundance, select words and pictures that symbolize the concept—photos of dollar bills, baskets of food, a phrase like *debt-free*, or whatever resonates with you best.

In the past, many people made vision boards with words and images cut from magazines, but not everyone buys magazines anymore—that's okay! Find images, phrases, and photos online and print them out. Arrange them in a collage on your foundation surface—take your time with it, getting them exactly where you like them. While you're doing so, reflect on your goal, and visualize it happening; don't just wish or hope for it, but actually *see* it manifesting. When you've got everything just right, glue your articles in place. Hang your vision board in a place where you can see it daily. The more you look at it and are reminded of your long-term goals, the closer you will come to manifesting your dreams.

Keep a Gratitude Journal

The Libra witch understands how important gratitude is—after all, our Sun sign falls at the halfway point of the astrological year, associated with balance and reflection. A great way to honor that balanced energy is to reflect upon the things we're grateful for, in order to attract more for us to appreciate. You'll soon discover the benefits of gratitude journaling, including a better sense of self-awareness and new clarity about the abundance you're manifesting in your life.

To start, get a brand-new journal for yourself. Pick out one that's aesthetically pleasing to you, if possible. We Libras like pretty things, so find one that reflects your vibe. You might even wish to buy a special, fancy pen for journaling. If you don't like writing things down and you're more of a digital person, think about keeping your journal on an app that's easily accessible from your phone or laptop so you can access it anytime the muse hits you.

Each day, or at other regular intervals, write down something you're thankful for. What is it, and *why* are you grateful for it? Are there ways you can share your appreciation with others? If you're intimidated by the look and feel of an empty page, no worries. Try a couple of simple prompts to get started:

+ Pick a photo from a time you were happy and write about it.
+ Reflect on a time someone said something kind to you, and how it made you feel.
+ Is there a musician or artist whose work inspires you? Journal about one of their songs or paintings, and why you love it.
+ Think about the last time you laughed and describe what brought you such joy.
+ Who is the person you trust the most in the world? Write them a thank-you note for being in your life.

+ Describe a time when you helped someone else
  with a simple act of kindness. How did you feel
  afterward?

Just like any other practice, keeping a journal is one that gets easier to maintain if we make it a habit. While you may not feel like doing it daily, try to do it at least a few times a week. Once you get into a regular routine, writing in your journal won't feel like a chore—it will be something you look forward to anytime something positive happens in your life.

Libra Creativity Magic

Creativity and magic go hand in hand; some of the most powerful spells and rituals we can perform are enhanced by our art, whatever form it may take. In knot magic, a spell is cast by tying a series of knots—when the final knot is tied, the spell is complete. You can do the same thing with your art or music or handcrafts. Every act of creation can be magical and transformative, so think about what direction your imagination can take. Do you paint? Sketch? Write poetry? Do you crochet, knit, weave, or sew? Perhaps you sing or play a musical instrument.

Consider the repetitive rhythm you feel when you run a brush over a canvas or loop a pair of needles with soft yarn. Think about the hypnotic power of putting words on paper, banging a drum, or sculpting a figure from damp clay. What is your artistic superpower? Is there a skill you'd like to learn? Now's your chance!

Focus on your intention: What is your magical goal, and what is its purpose? Begin your artistic endeavor—sing a song or verbalize a chant, get out your paints or markers and start a picture, whip out that fiber and begin weaving or sewing. Whatever project you choose to create, use it as a catalyst for your magical intention. With each stitch or brushstroke or word or musical note, visualize your path to your goal growing stronger, building along with your project. Continue until your project—your poem, your song, your scarf, your drawing—is complete; when you've finished the creation, the spell work is done, and manifestation can begin.

A Spell for Bringing Ideas to Fruition

Kelden

Part of being an air sign is having a penchant for mental inspiration, and part of being a Libra is the natural inclination to see multiple perspectives. While this can be a wonderful thing, it can also make choosing an idea and determining the steps to manifest it difficult. The following spell calls upon the powers of air, as well as earth, to help you pick an idea and bring it to fruition.

You will need:

+ A stick of your favorite incense and a holder
+ A small feather
+ A medium bowl of dirt
+ A pen and two sheets of paper

To begin, light your incense in its holder. Place the bowl of dirt on a table or another low surface and set the incense next to it. Next, hold the feather in your hand. Every feather contains its own unique spirit, so take a moment to kindly ask for its assistance with this spell. Whisper to the feather your ideas and your desire for one of them to take hold. Close your eyes and call upon the element of air, the element of inspiration. Take in a nice inhale, breathing in some of the incense smoke. Imagine a soft wind blowing across your brow, bringing with it the virtues of clarity. When you're ready, recite the following incantation:

On the winds, ideas do fly
But one must land now, by and by
Called down it is, sowed in the earth
From stone and mud, form shall give birth
Thus, from my mind, a tree does root
One idea, turned into fruit

Holding the feather above the bowl, let go and allow it to fall through the incense smoke, landing upon the dirt. Using your hands, take up some of the dirt and cover the feather completely. As you do this, call upon the element of earth. Imagine that from the dirt, a tree begins to sprout, giving form to your once abstract idea.

Your spell is in motion; it's time to get to work on choosing an idea and fleshing it out. Using your pen and paper, list out all your ideas. Once completed, take a moment to look over the list. Notice which idea you are drawn to the most. On a second piece of paper, write down the idea you've chosen and answer the following questions:

1. What do you like about this idea? What about this particular idea inspires or excites you? Why is this idea personally important to you?

2. What do you need (time, energy, knowledge, money, etc.)? Do you have access to those resources or know where/how to obtain them? If not, you may need to select another idea.

3. What action steps can you take to move forward? How can you break the process down? What are your bigger goals, and what are the smaller goals that can help you achieve them?

When you've finished writing, place your papers underneath the bowl (you might want to move the bowl to a place where it will be undisturbed). Get to work, following your action steps. Return to the bowl of dirt as needed to review your writing and to connect with the balanced virtues of air and earth. When your idea has fully taken form, you may discard the dirt and feather as you see fit.

MAGICAL
CORRESPONDENCES
Patti Wigington

♎

As a Libra witch, whether you're a seasoned veteran or a "new-bie," you'll figure out that there are some magical practices and types of spells you're naturally drawn to. Here's a quick primer on some of the magical activities Libra witches find most effective, magical tools, and ideas for magical intentions that align well with Libra's balanced, harmonious energy. For instance, if you wanted to create a spell for justice, you might consider writing a letter on yellow paper to the universe. For beauty magic, you could call out a chant in front of a mirror.

Types of Spellcraft

+ Creativity magic
+ Meditation and visualization
+ Air element magic
+ Divination and psychic work
+ Chants and incantations
+ Magical writing

Magical Tools

+ Divination items
+ Feathers and fans
+ Colors: yellow, white, blue
+ Brooms
+ Mirrors
+ Incense blends

Magical Goals and Spell Ideas

+ Spells for love and relationships
+ Justice spells
+ Beauty magic
+ Rituals for balance and harmony
+ Peacekeeping spells
+ Leadership and communication magic

TIMING, PLACES, AND THINGS

Ivo Dominguez, Jr.

You've probably encountered plenty of charts and lists in books and online, cataloging which things relate to your Sun sign and ruling planet. There are many gorgeously curated assortments of herbs, crystals, music playlists, fashions, sports, fictional characters, tarot cards, and more that are assigned to your Sun sign. These compilations of associations are more than a curiosity or for entertainment. Correspondences are like treasure maps to show you where to find the type and flavor of power you are seeking. Correspondences are flowcharts and diagrams that show the inner occult relationship between subtle energies and the physical world. Although there are many purposes for lists of correspondences, there are two that are especially valuable to becoming a better Libra witch.

The first is to contemplate the meaning of the correspondences, the ways in which they reveal meaningful details about your Sun sign and ruling planet, and how they connect to you. This will deepen your understanding of what it is to be a Libra witch.

The second is to use these items as points of connection to access energies and essences that support your witchcraft. This will expand the number of tools and resources at your disposal for all your efforts.

Each of the sections in this chapter will introduce you to a type of correlation with suggestions on how to identify and use it. These are just starting points, and you will find many more as you explore and learn. As you broaden your knowledge, you may find yourself a little bit confused as you find that sources disagree on the correlations. These contradictions are generally not a matter of who is in error but a matter of perspective, cultural differences, and the intended uses for the correlations. Anything that exists in the physical world can be described as a mixture of all the elements, planets, and signs. You may be a Libra, but depending on the rest of your chart, there may be strong concentrations of other signs and elements. For example, if you find that a particular herb is listed as associated with both Libra and Taurus, it is because it contains both natures in abundance. In the cases of strong multiple correlations, it is important to summon or tune in to the one you need.

Times

You always have access to your power as a Libra witch, but there are times when the flow is stronger, readily available, or more easily summoned. There are sophisticated astrological methods to select dates and times that are specific to your birth chart. Unless you want to learn quite a bit more astrology or hire someone to determine these for you, you can do quite well with simpler methods. Let's look at the cycles of the solar year, the lunar month, and the hours of day-night rotation. When the Sun is in Libra, or the Moon is in Libra, or early in the evening just after sunset, you are in the sweet spot for tuning in to the core of your power.

Libra season is roughly September 23–October 22, but check your astrological calendar or ephemeris to determine when it is for a specific year in your time zone. The amount of accessible energy is highest when the Sun is at the same degree of Libra as it is in your birth chart. This peak will not always be on your birth date, but very close to it. Take advantage of Libra season for working magick and for recharging and storing up energy for the whole year.

The Moon moves through the twelve signs every lunar cycle and spends around two and half days in each sign. When the Moon is in Libra, you have access to more lunar power because the Moon in the heavens has a resonant link to the Sun in your birth chart. At some point during its time in Libra, the Moon will be at the same degree as your Sun. For you, that will be the peak of the energy during the Moon's passage through Libra that month. While the Moon is in Libra, your psychism is stronger, as is your ability to manifest things. When the Moon is a waning half Moon in any sign, you can draw upon its power more readily because it is resonant to your sign.

The Sun enters Libra at the autumn equinox in the northern hemisphere. The date for the autumn equinox varies because the calendar is not anchored to celestial events. The peak of Libra season is its midpoint at the fifteenth degree; this is a special day of power for you. You can look up when the Sun is in the fifteenth degree of Libra for the current or future years using online resources or an ephemeris. Libra is the seventh sign of the zodiac, and the zodiac is like a clock for the purposes of spell work. Early evening corresponds to the airy power of Libra. If you are detail focused, you might be wondering when early evening is. This varies with the time of year and with your location, but if you must have a time, think of it as 6:00 p.m. to 8:00 p.m. Or you can use your intuition and feel your way to when early evening is on any given day. The powers that flow during this time are rich, creative, and filled with possibilities for you to experience. Plan on using the Libra energy of the dusk and early evening to fuel and feed spells for harmony, divination, creativity, and fairness.

The effect of these special times can be joined in any combination. For example, you can choose to do work in the early evening when the Moon is in Libra, or when the Sun is in Libra at early evening, or when the Moon is in Libra during Libra season. You can combine all three as well. Each of these time period groupings will have a distinctive feeling. Experiment and use your instincts to discover how to use these in your work.

Places

There are activities, professions, phenomena, and behaviors that have an affinity, a resonant connection, to Libra and its ruling planet, Venus. These activities occur in the locations that suit or facilitate their expressions. There is magick to be claimed from those places that is earmarked for Libra or your ruling planet of Venus. Just like your birth chart, the world around you contains the influences of all the planets and signs, but in different proportions and arrangements. You can always draw upon Libra or Venus energy, though there are times when it is more abundant depending on astrological considerations. Places and spaces have energies that accumulate and can be tapped as well. Places contain the physical, emotional, and spiritual environments that are created by the actions of the material objects, plants, animals, and people occupying those spaces. Some of the interactions between these things can generate or concentrate the energies and patterns that can be used by Libra witches.

If you look at traditional astrology books, you'll find listings of places assigned to Libra and Venus that include locations such as these:

- Social clubs, tea and coffee shops, cozy or opulent eateries
- Spas, yoga centers, dance studios
- Group art or craft sessions and craft shows
- Vineyards, botanical gardens, flower shows

These are very clearly linked to the themes associated with Libra and Venus. With a bit of brainstorming and free-associating, you'll find many other less obvious locations and situations where you can draw upon this power. For example, a games night, sightseeing with friends, or attending an interfaith event can produce a current you can plug into. Any mentally *and* emotionally stimulating activity—planning for an event, decorating for a holiday, cooking together, or similar activities—can become a source of power for a Libra witch. All implements or actions related to the creative arts, decor, cuisine, and many more situations also could be a source for energy.

While you can certainly go to places that are identified as locations where Libra and/or Venus's energy is plentiful to do workings, you can find those energies in many other circumstances. Don't be limited by the idea that the places must be the ones that have a formalized link to Libra. Be on the lookout for Libra or Venus themes and activities wherever you may be. Remember that people thinking, feeling, or participating in activities connected to your sign and its ruling planet are raising power. If you can identify with it as resonating with your Sun sign or ruling planet, then you can call the power and put it to use. You complete the circuit to engage the flow with your visualization, intentions, and actions.

Plants

Libra is airy and sophisticated, arranges things to maximize beauty, and is elegant; its colors are pink, lavender, and light blue (though most pastels work). Venus adds a focus on enjoying the senses, attracting people, and reveling in the bliss of just existing. Herbs, resins, oils, fruits, vegetables, woods, and flowers that strongly exhibit one or more of these qualities can be called upon to support your magick. Here are a few examples:

- ◎ Magnolia because its scent gives emotional perseverance.

- ◎ Roses, especially pink ones, to release outworn attitudes and worries.

◎) Black cohosh for restoring balance to the body.

◎) Chicory for getting back a lost or broken heart.

◎) Vervain for keeping good boundaries and averting evil.

Once you understand the rationale for making these assignments, the lists of correspondences will make more sense. Another thing to consider is that each part of a plant may resonate more strongly with a different element, planet, and sign. Damiana shows its connection with Libra and Venus through its pastel yellow flowers and its use as an aphrodisiac. However, damiana is also used as a fire herb associated with Jupiter for incense for scrying, trance, and visions. Which energy steps forward depends on your call and invitation. "Like calls to like" is a truism in witchcraft. When you use your Libra nature to make a call, you are answered by the Libra part of the plant.

Plant materials can take the form of incense, anointing oils, altar pieces, potions, washes, magickal implements, foods, flower arrangements, and so on. The mere presence of plant material that is linked to Libra or Venus will be helpful to you. However, to gain the most benefit from plant energy, you need to actively engage with it. Push some of your energy into the plants and then pull on it to start the flow. Although much of the plant material you work with will be dried or preserved, it retains a connection to living members of their species. You may also want to reach out and try to commune with the spirit, the group soul, of the plants to request their assistance or guidance. This will awaken the power slumbering in the dried or preserved plant material. Spending time with living plants—whether they be houseplants, in your yard, or in a public garden—will strengthen your conversation with the green beings under Libra's eye.

Crystals and Stones

Before digging into this topic, let's clear up some of the confusion around the birthstones for the signs of the zodiac. There are many varying lists for birthstones. Also be aware that some are related to the calendar month rather than the zodiacal signs. There are traditional lists, but the most commonly available lists for birthstones were created by jewelers to sell more jewelry. Also be cautious of the word *traditional* as some jewelers refer to the older lists compiled by jewelers as "traditional." The traditional lists created by magickal practitioners also diverge from each other because of cultural differences and the availability of different stones in the times and places the lists were created. If you have already formed a strong connection to a birthstone that you discover is not really connected to the energy of your sign, keep using it. Your connection is proof of its value to you in moving, holding, and shifting energy, whether or not it is specifically attuned to Libra.

These are my preferred assignments of birthstones for the signs of the zodiac:

Aries	Bloodstone, Carnelian, Diamond
Taurus	Rose Quartz, Amber, Sapphire
Gemini	Agate, Tiger's Eyes, Citrine
Cancer	Moonstone, Pearl, Emerald
Leo	Heliodor, Peridot, Black Onyx
Virgo	Green Aventurine, Moss Agate, Zircon
Libra	Jade, Lapis Lazuli, Labradorite
Scorpio	Obsidian, Pale Beryl, Nuummite
Sagittarius	Turquoise, Blue Topaz, Iolite
Capricorn	Black Tourmaline, Howlite, Ruby

Aquarius	Amethyst, Sugalite, Garnet
Pisces	Ametrine, Smoky Quartz, Aquamarine

There are many other possibilities that work just as well, and I suggest you find what responds best for you as an individual. I've included all twelve signs in case you'd like to use the stones for your Moon sign or rising sign. Hands-on experimentation is the best approach, so I suggest visiting crystal or metaphysical shops and rock and mineral shows when possible. Here's some information on the three I prefer for Libra:

Jade

Jade comes in many tasteful colors and gives stability and calming support. It helps to encourage self-reliance and reinforces your personal goals. This stone encourages you to not only listen to your intuitions, but to act on them. During troubled times, it can help you regain a broader perspective. When you are talking to people, jade helps you notice little clues that give insight into their thoughts and feelings. Jade is also good for balancing fluids in the body and the elimination of toxins. Jade works slowly and steadily, but its effects go deeper and last longer. All jade is good, but nephrite jade is the best for Libra.

Lapis Lazuli

Lapis lazuli activates your vision and your voice. It helps you tap into your deeper wiser self. This stone helps you speak truths, sometimes difficult ones, in loving ways that build rather than harm relationships. Lapis lazuli acts as a shield against hostile or stressful energies or atmospheres. It is especially good at deflecting the evil eye, envy, and ill wishes. As a healing stone, it feeds you energy in the amount that you can best use. If you do healing work, it will help sustain your energy and focus. This stone also encourages you to make a decision and move forward rather than revisiting the question. Focus on the glints of pyrite in the stone to connect with your higher Self.

Labradorite

This stone brings hidden thoughts and feelings to the surface so you can work with them. It also helps you dredge up old pains and hurts and facilitates their release. Labradorite stimulates the psychic senses and the imagination in a positive and healthy manner. It also stirs creativity and helps you connect with your muse. It is a stone of choosing your own destiny as it helps you see the best options at each fork in your path. It also is useful for exploring your past in this life and previous ones. Focus on the flashes of color in the stone to connect with your higher Self.

Intuition and spiritual guidance play a part in the making of correlations and, in the case of traditional lore, the collective experience of many generations of practitioners. There is also reasoning behind how these assignments are made, and understanding the process will help you choose well. Here are some examples of this reasoning:

- Crystals assigned to Libra are light, comforting colors or come in many varieties because they suggest Libra and Venus in their appearance. Peach moonstone, selenite, and kunzite are good examples.

- Libra's metal is copper, and stones that have significant amounts of copper, such as shattuckite, azurite, and chrysocolla, also work well for you.

- Crystals such as apophyllite, rhodonite, spirit quartz, and pink calcite, whose lore and uses are related to Libra or Venus actions or topics such as reconciliation, love, and self-love, are recommended as crystals for Libra.

- Crystals that are the opposite of the themes for Libra provide a counterbalance to an excessive manifestation of Libra traits. For example, red (almandine) garnet appears on lists of crystals for other signs but is useful for Libra for boosting bold and direct action.

◎ Crystals suggested for Aries, your opposite sign, are also useful to maintain your balance.

Working with Ritual Objects

A substantial number of traditions or schools of witchcraft use magickal tools that are consecrated to represent and hold the power of the elements. Oftentimes in these systems, there is one primary tool for each of the elements and other tools that are alternatives to these or are mixtures of elements. There are many possible combinations and reasons for why the elements are assigned to different tools in different traditions, and they all work within their own context. Find and follow what works best for you.

Magickal tools and ritual objects are typically cleansed, consecrated, and charged to prepare them for use. In addition to following whatever procedure you may have for preparing your tools, add in a step to incorporate your energy and identity as a Libra witch. This is especially productive for magickal tools and ritual objects that are connected to air or are used for centering work or to store or focus power. By adding Libra energy and patterning into the preparation of your tools, you will find it easier to raise, move, and shape energy with them in your workings.

There are many magickal tools and ritual objects that do not have any attachment to specific elements. The core of your life force and magickal power springs from your Libra Sun. So, when you consciously join your awareness of your Libra core with the power flowing through the tools or objects, it increases their effectiveness. Develop the habit of using the name *Libra* as a word of power, the glyph for Libra for summoning power, and the soft pastel colors of Libra to visualize its flow. Whether it be a pendulum, a wand, a crystal, or a chalice, your Libra energy will be quick to rise and answer your call.

A Charging Practice

When you consciously use your Libra witch energy to send power into tools, it tunes them more closely to your aura. Here's a quick method for imbuing any tool with your Libra energy.

1. Place the tool in front of you on a table or altar.
2. Take a breath in, imagining that you are breathing in pink or lavender energy, and then say "Libra" as you exhale. Repeat this three times.
3. Lift up your left forearm and hold it horizontally at the height of your gaze. Now use the index and middle finger of your right hand and trace a line of energy just above your forearm with a semicircle bumping up in the middle. You've just formed the glyph for Libra.
4. Now, using your fingers, trace the glyph of Libra over or on the tool you are charging. Repeat this several times and imagine the glyph being absorbed by the tool.

5. Pick up the tool, take in a breath while imaging pink or lavender energy, and blow that charged breath over the tool.
6. Say "Blessed be!" and proceed with using the tool or putting it away.

Hopefully this charging practice will inspire you and encourage you to experiment. Reinforce the habit of using the name *Libra* as a word of power, the glyph for Libra for summoning power, and the colors of Libra to visualize its flow. Feel free to use these spontaneously in all your workings. Whether it be a pendulum, a wand, a crystal, a chalice, a ritual robe, or anything else that catches your imagination, these simple methods can have a large impact. The Libra energy you imprint into them will be quick to rise and answer your call.

HERBAL
CORRESPONDENCES

♎

These plant materials all have a special connection to your energy as a Libra witch. There are many more, but these are a good starting point.

Herbs

Cardamom	for vitality and balanced energies
Elderberry	for healing and protection
Lady's Mantle	for clarity in your psychism

Flowers

Love in a Mist	for love, devotion, or deception
Brugmansia	for soul journeys and second sight
Nasturtium	strengthens hope and beliefs

Incense and Fragrances

Bergamot	to bring physical and emotional abundance
Galbanum Resin	to commune with good spirits
Frangipani	for restoring peace and connections

CLEANSING AND SHIELDING

Patti Wigington

Libras can be hyper-attuned to the emotions and needs of other people, although we often do a good job of hiding it from the rest of the world. In fact, we sometimes come off as aloof, because once we learn to set boundaries, we're pretty firm about not allowing anyone to cross them. We'll eagerly stand up for what we believe to be fair and right, and we'll do it in a way that's diplomatic and civil. Libras can also be very romantic souls—a Libra in a relationship is all in, 100 percent. But we also value loyalty, and once our trust is lost, it's very hard—and sometimes impossible— to gain it back. Honestly, a Libra witch can be somewhat of a paradox, revealing their true selves only to those they trust and care about. It's not that we live in a way that's inauthentic, it's just that we're a bit guarded about who we share our deepest thoughts and feelings with. You'll only learn as much about a Libra as they wish you to know, and no more.

Because a Libra can be a bit of a walking contradiction, it's important for us to remember our symbolic scales of balance—and it's easy to forget what they represent, because we're so darn busy all the time! But finding balance and harmony can get left in the dust if we allow ourselves to forget about clearing our space, removing toxic energy from our environment, and shielding ourselves from that which would do us harm.

Clear Your Energy Clutter

Libras are great listeners, and we make everyone who tells us their stories feel like they're the center of our world. We typically offer both support and solutions, and friends and family will sigh and tell us how easy we are to talk to. That's a great quality to have … but it also means you can pick up a whole lot of yuck from other people. Toxicity and negativity abound in our world, and if you don't shed them regularly (or, ideally, keep them at bay completely), you'll start to feel the harmful effects in your own mind, body, and spirit.

One of the best ways for Libras to clear toxic energy clutter is a two-pronged attack. First, learn to center by mindfully regulating your breathing—breath work is the foundation of many magical practices, and developing a habit of mindful breathing is a great way to push out any of that negativity you may have picked up from others. Begin by finding a quiet place where you can work without interruptions. Sit comfortably—or lie down, if you can do so without falling asleep—and take a long, slow, deep breath as you count to three. Wait for a moment, and then slowly exhale, again counting to three. Repeat this as many times as you need to, until you feel yourself calmed and relaxed.

As you continue to breathe mindfully, close your eyes and visualize all the parts of your body surrounded by soft light. Beginning with the crown of your head, pull the light into yourself. Inspect how it feels and looks to you inside your body. Work your way downward, slowly and thoughtfully, visualizing the light spreading in your throat, your heart, your arms, down into your torso, your legs, all the way to your toes. Does the light appear and feel centered and even? Excellent!

However, if you encounter a blockage, a dark spot, or just the sense that something is out of whack, envision the light moving toward that spot. See it filling you, pushing out any toxicity and negative energy with the light overtaking the darkness. Send the yuck away, far from your body and spirit. Continue until your entire body is full of light—nothing is off-kilter, nothing is out of place…each and every part of you is floating in a delicious, harmonious, and balanced space.

In addition to metaphysical cleansing, it's helpful to ritually cleanse the body physically as well. We Libras really like luxury and relaxation, so a good long soak can be incredibly advantageous on a physical, spiritual, and emotional level.

Fill your bathtub with warm water—you may even want to add a few scented candles around the space or turn on some of your favorite soft music for extra self-pampering. Add a cup of sea salt and a cup of baking soda to the water. Climb into the tub, immersing yourself, and close your eyes. Use a fresh washcloth or loofah sponge to wash your body, visualizing any toxic energy or negativity being scrubbed away. Start with your forehead and work gradually, all the way to your toes, moving the washcloth downward each time. Once you're completely clean—as an added bonus, your skin will have a nice glow!—drain the tub and let anything toxic that you've shed go right down the drain. Don't just visualize it—*see* it.

If you don't have a bathtub, don't worry! Use a bowl or sink full of warm water and a soft, clean washcloth, and you can do the same exercise. Begin with your head, work your way down to your toes, and when you're finished, either drain the sink or take the bowl of water outside for disposal.

Shielding and Energetic Boundary Setting

Learning to shield is one of the most powerful and protective actions a Libra witch can take. Remember, many people misinterpret our natural sense of balance as wishy-washiness—and they may try to take advantage of it. By shielding, you can protect yourself from negative energy, toxic people, psychic attack, and any number of other metaphysical crises.

There are several different ways to shield, and whichever one you choose, get in the habit of doing it regularly—after a while, it will become instinctive, and you won't even have to give it a lot of thought. It will just happen naturally, offering protection in any setting.

Try visualizing the thing that makes you feel most protected. Is it a big stone wall you can stand behind? A suit of armor or a cloak of power? Perhaps it's your ancestors and your spirit guides, holding fast in front of you. Whatever it may be, practice calling it into position when you don't actually need it—it's a great way to prepare for the times it will be necessary. Close your eyes and see your wall—or your armor—surrounding you. Don't just see it, though. Feel it. Reach out and touch the solid bricks of your spiritual fortress; feel how cool and strong they are beneath your touch. If you see yourself wearing armor, sense its weight on your body—firm and unyielding. Hear the *clank* as you tap on your chest plate. Make your shielding *real*.

Another method you can use is by invoking a shield of light—again, you'll want to learn to do this before you actually have to use it. Close your eyes, regulate your breathing, and envision a powerful light right above the crown of your head. What color is your light? Is it pink, filling you with love? Red or purple, to reclaim your power? Perhaps it's yellow or white, connecting you to the air of the Libra Sun sign. Slowly, gradually, picture your light spreading downward,

surrounding the outside of your body like a cocoon, form-
ing a bubble from your head to your feet. Now imagine it
expanding outward, growing stronger and more solid, until
you are completely enveloped in its safety. The more you do
this, the easier it will become. Practice working with your
shield of light while you're alone, and then you'll be able to
do it without much thought at all when you're around other
people.

If you don't have the time for a full shielding routine
every single time, don't panic—there are other quick and
simple preventative practices that work well for Libras!

◎ Carry a grounding stone or crystal with you, either
   in your pocket or worn as a piece of jewelry. Black
   tourmaline, obsidian, or hematite work well to
   protect us from negativity and restore balance.
   When you're feeling run-down or surrounded by
   toxicity, let the stone absorb that energy and take
   the hit for you.

◎ Remember the power of air signs—wind can create, and it can destroy. If you're about to enter an
   environment where you know you'll be in contact with people whose energy could be draining,
   as you walk in, visualize yourself surrounded by
   a powerful wind that can blow away any hostility,

toxicity, or negative behavior that comes your way.

◎) Wear or carry a piece of copper. Associated with Venus, copper can be used to deflect negative energy. As an added bonus, it's also connected to powers of communication, so perhaps you can take advantage of a negative situation by using your natural skills of diplomacy to diffuse the matter at hand and bring about harmony and balance.

In addition to shielding, it's perfectly acceptable—actually, no, scratch that … it's *healthy*, to set energetic boundaries. This means *you* get to choose whose energy you share and accept. Each and every one of us is allowed to establish our personal safety bubble, and we don't have to let anyone into it we don't want there. If there's someone in your life who's constantly bringing you down, bombarding you with rage and hostility, you're allowed to eliminate them from your circle. If that's not really an option—after all, we don't choose our family or coworkers—the alternative is to set firm boundaries. It's healthy and empowering to look at someone, right in the eye, and say, "I will not allow you to speak like this around/to/at me." Repeat as many times as you have to until they get the message.

Magic to Be Mindful Of

One thing that most Libra witches learn very early in our practice is that it's important to learn from our mistakes. You may find that certain types of spells have a less-than-positive impact on your emotions and spirit, so it's important to take precautions when these matters arise.

The typical Libra witch may not be consumed by their appearance; in fact, we often value comfort over style, yet other people still find themselves drawn to us. However, we do like things to look nice, and that includes ourselves. Be cautious in doing beauty spells—you don't want to get so caught up in the process that you come across as vain or self-absorbed. When that happens, other people may view you differently, and not in a good way … and that's the *last* thing a Libra wants.

Because Libras are talented at working with people of all different backgrounds and social styles, we sometimes find ourselves in the middle of experiences where we're in complete control of a situation, but happy to let other people take the credit and glory. If you're doing spell work to nudge a collaborative project along, be careful—there's a difference between influencing people and manipulating them. Be mindful in your magic, and make sure you're not taking advantage of other people simply because they're eager to listen to you.

You may even find certain locations affect the way your magic works. Libras love socializing…but only on our own terms, and sometimes in small doses. We also dislike clutter and chaos. So, if you find yourself attempting to work magic or perform a ritual in a place that seems crowded, loud, noisy, or just sheer madness, you need to walk away. No matter how experienced a practitioner you are, disruptive people or environments can get inside the head of a Libra witch. You might also feel jittery and anxious, like you've lost control of the situation. When that happens, you may find your magic fails to be effective, which will cause you to second-guess your abilities later. Give yourself a break and take advantage of the Libra's natural tendency toward patience; you can do your magical work another time, another place, when there isn't so much pandemonium.

Libras tend to burn out if we don't take care of ourselves, so if you just don't have the mental bandwidth to handle a task—be it magical or mundane—set it aside until you're feeling better, physically, mentally, and spiritually.

WHAT SETS A LIBRA OFF, AND HOW TO RECOVER

Patti Wigington

The typical Libra is pretty even-keeled—we don't get super worked up about things that annoy us, although we may spend a lot of time in our own heads reviewing all the things we dislike about the situation. For the most part, we try to be objective and understand that people have multiple viewpoints, even if we thoroughly disagree with them or think they're ridiculous. But never fear, there's good news! In typical Libra fashion, we can take those situations, reflect upon them, and then learn valuable lessons from our Sun sign to help us move forward. Once we become aware of what gets on our last nerve, and *why*, it's a whole lot easier to deal—and because we like balance, we can view these experiences as not rants or venting sessions, but as opportunities to move forward in a way that's healthy and beneficial to us.

Unnecessary Conflict

I have a love-hate relationship with social media. On the one hand, it's a great way for me to stay connected with friends and family all over the world. I can share something with the click of a button rather than emailing a photo of my cats to hundreds of people individually. I can engage in conversations—both of the lighthearted fun variety, and those of a more serious, deep nature—with people whose opinions I value and respect. On the flip side, social media platforms can also be a place of absolutely outrageous conflict and aggression. We've all seen people pick fights with random strangers just because they were able to do so behind the anonymity of their laptop or phone screen. And it drives me bonkers.

Frankly, it's exhausting for many Libras, because while we enjoy and value social interaction, we tend to hate conflict that exists just for the sake of existing. So how do we keep our equilibrium between staying engaged and stepping away when the drama llamas have us ready to tear our own hair out, making us want to just *nope?*

Remember how much Libras value balance? This is where self-care comes in. If you're comfortable saying yes to things you like, then you can also be comfortable saying no to things you don't. That includes social interaction if it's making you feel bad rather than boosting your spirits. You don't have to get involved in every conversation you see—and if people ask you to weigh in on something, you don't have to if you don't have the mental bandwidth for it. I have one social media acquaintance who always sends me links to arguments she's having, saying, "Look at this nonsense, you should jump in here and say something!" No. I really shouldn't. Because I don't have to fight every single battle that other people are having on the internet.

About three times a year, I take a deliberate break from social media. I don't announce it to anyone—it's not an airport, no one needs to hear about my departure. I just go dark for a week or so. I remove my social apps from my phone and tablet, log out of everything on my laptop, and treat myself to a social media hiatus. Usually, I know it's time to come back when friends begin texting or calling me to make sure I'm not dead. When I return, I'm in a far better headspace, and typically I discover nothing burned down while I was away.

Clutter and Disorganization

I love order and can't thrive in an environment full of chaos; a lack of structure tends to make me anxious. If a physical space is cluttered, noisy, and disorganized, my brain follows suit, and while I may be "doing things," I accomplish exactly 100 percent of nothing, which in turn drives me bananas; Libras like to get stuff done, and we hate it when we can't or don't. When I begin mistaking activity for productivity,

I know it's time to evaluate the space I'm occupying and find ways to make it more conducive to harmony.

One of my few possessions that I love the most is my late grandfather's desk. It's where I do my work each day for my full-time corporate job, and it's where I write, pay bills, and stay organized. It's also enormous—it's a good six feet long and three feet deep (I know, because I had to measure it to make sure it would fit through the door when I bought a house) and has all kinds of cool little cubbies and drawers. And because it's so darn big, it often becomes a place where I pile things I need to tackle later. After all, if it's something that needs to be filed, addressed, or responded to, the desk is the perfect place, right? Until I realize I've gotten so busy doing other things that I now have three different stacks of paper piled up on my desk begging for my attention. I've looked at them on the daily, reminded myself I need to do something with them … but not actually *done* anything.

Combine these feral piles of paper with the dust that accumulates in a century-old house, and the random clumps of fur generated by two cats who lack boundaries, and pretty soon my desk is a disaster zone. And it's a place where I can no longer focus, which of course makes me even more frustrated.

So now, on the first Sunday of each month, I spend about thirty minutes to an hour organizing my desk. I take everything off the surface; top to bottom, I dust and polish (and vacuum up the cat fluffles); and I file any bits of paper that need to be put away, taking care of the tasks I've been avoiding. It's a tiny amount of time invested, but the end result is that my desk is once again manageable and clean, other than my laptop, monitor, a few family photos, and a basket of pens.

If you find yourself overwhelmed by *stuff*—or at the very least, stuff that isn't where it's supposed to be—take a few moments out of your morning on a regular basis and get it gone. If it seems like too overwhelming of a job to do all at once, do it in small chunks: One day, dust. The next day, throw away things you don't have to keep. The following day, file or put away.

As much as I hate tidying up, I dislike the chaos of a messy space even more.

Rude and Unkind People

Much like unnecessary conflict, most Libras get set off by rudeness or unkindness. There's an awful lot of both of these things in the world right now, and since Libras tend to be sensitive to the emotions of others, we *feel* it when we see uncivilized behavior. We don't want to go along with the whole "if you can't beat 'em, join 'em" mentality—Libras don't have it in us to be deliberately mean. But we *can* be pretty strong when we see things that are unfair, and we can address it in ways that are determined and confident while staying true to our natures. One thing that can be incredibly beneficial to the Libra witch is exploring the traits of our Sun sign opposite—in our case, it's the sign of Aries.

The typical Aries is courageous and driven, generous and passionate, much like Libras. However, the Aries sign is far more immediately action driven than we Libras—and they also tend to care far less than we do about what others think of them. By embracing a bit of Aries energy, we can address unkindness or mean-spirited behavior in the moment, rather than stewing on it and coming up with really great responses long after the situation has ended.

For many years, I worked as a department lead for a major bookselling chain. If you've ever worked retail, you know sometimes shopping brings out the worst in people, and I saw it on a regular basis. While it was rarely directed at me personally—and if it had been, I'd have just pulled a classic Generation X *meh, whatever* and wandered off—I began to see it directed at my younger, inexperienced coworkers. One year, during the holiday season, two cashiers quit in a single week, after particularly nasty customers made them cry. At first, I didn't think there was anything I could do about it—but then I realized the unfairness of it all. These kids were just trying to do their jobs during the most stressful time of the year, and here they had fully grown adults being horrible to them at work.

I decided it was time to let my Libra energy channel my inner Aries. I told the cashiers, "If someone is being mean to you, let me know, and I will handle it." Sure enough, I became the person the seasonal kids relied on for assistance, because when customers got ugly, I simply addressed them with, "I understand you are frustrated and possibly even angry about something, but I will absolutely *not* allow you to be abusive to anyone who works here, and that is final." By politely acknowledging their frustration with holiday shopping, I allowed my Libra voice to speak up and do its thing, but I let my Aries energy explain, right then and there, that their bad behavior would not be tolerated. Although I occasionally got yelled at—in which case the customer was told to leave the store completely—I was nearly always able to diffuse the situation.

I've discovered that when someone's crappy behavior toward others is putting me on edge, I can be firm and fair at the same time—and that combination of Libra and Aries traits has served me very well in the years since.

The Power of the Queens Spell

Emma Kathyrn

This spell seeks to gather the power of the Queens combined. Libran witches often spend a lot of time and effort helping others, sometimes forgoing their own self-care in the process, so this spell is about taking time for yourself, about manifesting your own reality in each area of your life—whatever that looks like for you.

You will need:

+ The four Queens from a tarot deck
+ Safe working space
+ Working altar
+ Candle, any color
+ Bowl of water
+ Cauldron or fireproof dish
+ Paper and a pen

Instructions:

You don't need a full spring-clean, but start by making the area you'll work in tidy so you feel more in control of the space. Set up your altar as you normally would. If you do not usually have an altar, then designate a space where you can place the cards and the other items required, letting your

own aesthetic tastes dictate
how that might look.

Sit before the lit candle and
bowl of water, holding the Queen cards
in your hand. Spend a few moments in
meditation, focusing on your breathing. There's
no need to change your breathing; simply notice each
breath and the sensations within your body.

Next, it's time to lay out the cards. Starting with the Queen
of Pentacles, lay it faceup on your altar or ground, saying,

Queen of Pentacles, Earth in the North,
The power of creation, the strength to grow.

Now, taking the Queen of Wands and placing it directly
beneath the Queen of Earth, say,

Queen of Wands, Fire in the South,
The power of illumination, the strength to destroy.

Lay down the Queen of Cups, placing it to the left of the
previous two cards so it forms the arm of a cross and say,

Queen of Cups, Water in the West,
The power of purification, the strength to satisfy.

Place the final card, the Queen of Swords, to the right so
that the cards together form a cross. Say,

Queen of Swords, Air in the East,
The power of communication, the strength to fell.
Power of the Queens combined,
Bring to me what shall be mine.
With these words, harken to me,
As I will it, so shall it be.

On your piece of paper, write down what it is you need. It might be a tangible thing, or a quality you wish to embody. It might just be an ear to listen to you, in which case, write down whatever is in your heart. I advise writing without censoring yourself, which can be harder to do than you think. This is the time and place to center yourself and your own needs, suspending any self-criticism or judgment.

Fold the paper and hold it to the candle's flame, allowing it to burn away in your cauldron. Take the ashes outside and hold them up to the wind, chanting,

Power of the Queens combined,
Bring to me what is mine.

When the ashes have blown away, go back inside. Have a drink of water and a bite to eat to help the grounding process, and that's it! May the power of the Queens combined bring all you wish for yourself!

A BRIEF BIO OF LEO MARTELLO

* * *

Manny Tejada y Moreno

Dr. Leo Louis Martello (1931–2000) was an author, hypnotist, graphologist, *mago*, and witch as well as a luminary within transgressive movements who leveraged all the Libra blessings and gifts for charm, balance, and justice. Leo entered the Craft through Gardnerian Wicca but also by embracing his Italian/Sicilian ancestral practice of witchcraft, later helping instigate its resurgence as Stregheria.

I met Leo—and only briefly—at the Magickal Childe in New York City during the height of the Satanic Panic and AIDS crisis of the mid-1980s. I thought he was a charming older homeless man outside the store. We didn't talk long, but he made some clever comment that made me feel welcome and calm, given that moment in history, being a young gay man from the Florida wild in an unfamiliar city at an occult shop. Leo sized me up quickly so I could enjoy my brief visit to the store while in the presence of its mercurial owner, Herman Slater, who, I learned much later, was his partner.

Unaware and soon-to-be-educated, I would learn Leo was an elder in two communities I knew well. He was a member of the Gay Liberation Front (GLF) and a writer for *Come Out!*, an LGBT newspaper from the GLF. He was also a well-known witch and *mago* in the Pagan community who leveraged his celebrity to advance the rights of both communities.

Libras are natural peacemakers and negotiators. They can see complexity easily, and Leo consistently cut through the fog of arguments used to oppress. Leo did both, while also guided by another distinctly Libra trait: a sense of justice.

Leo was the first to describe how the atrocities of the Salem Witch Trials continued to plague American society into the twentieth century. He could see, and more importantly, connect the thread to history that led to Pagan discrimination even today. He even sought damages to be paid by the Vatican and the Commonwealth of Massachusetts. Leo's uncompromising work on behalf of our rights turned him into an elder statesman of the Pagan community in the 1980s.

Leo could see—in a quintessentially Libran way—the path to balance through equity and equality. He foresaw how the Civil Rights Act of 1964 could be used to establish Pagan temples. He called for a National Witches' Day Parade. He led a witch-in at Central Park that led to the creation of the Witches Antidefamation League (later renamed the Witches Anti-Discrimination Lobby) to secure the religious rights of witches and Pagans. He also created the Witches International Craft Associates to create networks among witches and Wiccans.

Leo also had that little-known Libra characteristic of being impatient. He had an urgency about justice, not only about Pagan rights, but about access to medication for those living with AIDS, and about the right to be gay without harassments or legal constraints about who you love. As Leo famously said, "Out of your broom closets and on to your brooms!"[2]

---

2. Leo Louis Martello, *Weird Ways of Witchcraft* (San Francisco: Red Wheel Weiser, 2011), v.

A Sampling of Libra Occultists

T. THORN COYLE
author, musician, dancer, and witch
(September 24, 1965)

ALEISTER CROWLEY
magician, author, and founder of Thelema
(October 12, 1875)

PATRICIA CROWTHER
author and one of the founders of Wicca
(October 14, 1927)

NEVILL DRURY
editor, author, and occultist
(October 1, 1947)

ALLAN KARDEC
author and educator on Spiritism
(October 3, 1804)

KATRINA MESSENGER
author and founder of Reflections Mystery School
(October 22, 1955)

THE SWAY OF YOUR MOON SIGN

Ivo Dominguez, Jr.

The Moon is the reservoir of your emotions, thoughts, and all your experiences. The Moon is your subconscious, your unconscious, and your instinctive response in the moment. The Moon is also the author, narrator, and the musical score in the ongoing movie in your mind that summarizes and mythologizes your story. The Moon is like a scrying mirror, a sacred well, that gives answers to the question of the meaning of your life. The style and the perspective of your Moon sign shapes your story, a story that starts as a reflection of your Sun sign's impetus. The remembrance of your life events is a condensed subjective story, and it is your Moon sign that summarizes and categorizes the data stream of your life.

In witchcraft, the Moon is our connection and guide to the physical and energetic tides in nature, the astral plane, and other realities. The Moon in the heavens as it moves through signs and phases also pulls and pushes on your aura. The Moon in your birth chart reveals the intrinsic qualities and patterns in your aura, which affects the form your magick takes. Your Sun sign may be the source of your essence and power, but your Moon sign shows how you use that power in your magick. This chapter describes the twelve possible arrangements of Moon signs with a Libra Sun and what each combination yields.

Moon in Aries

You are courageous, inventive, and often inspiring to other people. If you see a task that needs to get done, you do it and do it quickly. You seem friendly and accommodating, but people eventually discover that inside you are as tough as nails. You are more independent and a bit quirkier than other Libras. You are likely to be drawn to ideas and practices that are far from mainstream, even in the witchcraft community. Solitude and solo activities are more important to you than the classic Libra. You are a mixture of conflicting natures, which can generate unique insights or make it harder to find a stable balance. Aries Moon makes you more prone to taking on an active role in creating fairness and justice. You like to juggle too many things at once, and if you add one too many and they begin to fall, your stress can be extreme. Ask for help; you've built up a long list of favors owed to you for all you've done.

You need to have several categories of friends so that you'll have a pool to draw on when you have a spontaneous urge to do something. This fiery Moon makes you light up when you want to draw people into your plans. You are not domestic nor domesticated, so your partners need to be energetic people with plans and goals of their own. They also need to be able to hold their own and say no as you can be too much. Boredom or externally imposed limits make you chafe. It is a danger sign when you start stirring things up just to see what happens. Take a break when this happens. Your thoughts are fast, and you are very perceptive, but that speedy flow also makes it harder to retain orderly memories. Note-taking, calendars, and recordings are your friend.

An Aries Moon, like all the fire element Moons, easily stretches forth to connect with the energy of other beings. The fiery qualities cleanse and protect your aura from picking up other people's emotional debris or being influenced by your environment. It is relatively easy for you to blend your energy with others and to separate cleanly. Your Libra Sun uses this rising's characteristics to extend the range of your charismatic pull, your psychism, and your fluency in giving readings. This combination assists in seeing all the forces and influences at play in spells and works.

Moon in Taurus

Both Libra and Taurus are ruled by Venus, so you get a double dose of that magick. You are a smooth operator, a charmer, and a bit of a hedonist. Your personal magnetism will attract people to join you in your work, quests, and adventures. The good news is that most people will enjoy or benefit from being pulled along with you. This combination tends to have strong romanticized and idealized thoughts about perfect partners, perfect living situations, and so on. If you use these thoughts as examples to strive for, all is well. If you use these as expectations, then you'll suffer a goodly amount of heartache. You generally believe in second chances for yourself and others. In a crisis situation, this Moon gives you common sense and stability. Others trust you instinctively when you take charge.

That Taurus Moon also encourages you to turn your ideas into expressions that are lasting and tangible. This could mean creating poetry, art, architecture, a perennial garden, or almost anything else that others can experience. You would be good at selling or teaching, or anything where you are changing hearts and minds. The Moon is said to be exalted in Taurus, which gives it greater power to add more poise and centeredness to your personality. It makes you more determined to trek onward until your goals are reached. You love to be supportive, but be mindful that your support does not cross the line into being meddlesome. If you find yourself slowing down or getting stuck in the same circumstances, spending time outdoors in nature is your best restorative. Another option is hosting a small social gathering or meal in your home.

A Taurus Moon, like all the earth element Moons, generates an aura that is magnetic and pulls energy inward. This Moon also makes it easier to create strong shields and wards. The auras of people with a Taurus Moon are excellent at holding or restoring a pattern or acting as a container or vessel in a working. You do well acting as a summoner or a vessel to attract spirits to you; you are the destination rather than the traveler to their realms. You have an aptitude for communicating with the Fae, nature spirits, and elementals. Take care that you fully release those connections when you are done. You also have a knack for fertility magick, plant magick, and attracting what you need.

♊

Moon in Gemini

A double dose of air energy makes you a talker, a thinker, and a daydreamer. You are energetic, lively, and often your tongue can't keep in sync with your speeding mind. You communicate several ideas at once, which can come out as brilliant or confusing depending on the listener. Learn to match your timing with your audience. When you get it right, your presence and eloquence are peerless. You feel more comfortable when you know the rules, vibe, expectations, and customs of the settings you are in. Be more direct in getting this background information. It is important to allocate your resources wisely because you love doing several things at once. You are brilliant, adaptable, and original, but time is a limited resource. If the cake recipe says to bake for an hour at a certain temperature, you can't have cake in thirty minutes by doubling the temperature. Physical activity and intellectual stimulation are the air you breathe; both are essential. Working with your hands is therapeutic for you.

Because you are so easygoing and gregarious, it can be hard to tell if you are flirting, being friendly, doing professional networking, and so on. Make sure you get the right message across. Just as importantly, don't lose yourself in your relationships. Don't let your desire for approval or praise keep you from pursuing your agenda. Your sharp intellect does have the power to see from various perspectives and reconsider situations to put head and heart in order. The people closest to you need to be easygoing, free spirited, and understanding of your changeable moods and interests. You are witty and appreciate humor. Watching comedies, comedians, cartoons, and so on is a great way to clear out the blues.

A Gemini Moon, like all the air Moons, makes it easier to engage in soul travel and psychism and gives the aura greater flexibility. When air aura reaches out and touches something, it can quickly read and copy the patterns it finds. A Gemini Moon gives the capacity to quickly adapt and respond to changing energy conditions in working magick or using the psychic senses. A wind can pick up and carry dust and debris, and the same is true for an aura. If you need to cleanse your energy, become as still as you can, and the debris will simply fall out of your aura. You are good at writing invocations, spells, and rituals with a special knack for finding things and restoring vitality.

Moon in Cancer

This Moon deepens your capacity to feel, identify, and analyze emotions. You are more aware of your emotions and other people's feelings than most other Libras. This combination lets you be a chameleon, a shape-shifter, who can blend into a social milieu. Your adaptability and social fluency allow you to hear a lot and garner influence and respect from a wide range of people. The Moon rules Cancer, which gives it a stronger shaping influence on your psyche and magick. Cancer Moon makes you want more security and stability than is usual for a Libra. You like to apply your creative flair and energy to make a calm and attractive home. So long as you are discerning in your choice of friends and associates, you can be very successful in life. You are good-hearted but can fail to notice systemic societal issues clearly. Shift your gaze from just individuals and look at groups of people, institutions, and cultures, and you'll see what needs attention. You have great adaptability, but that does not mean you have to fit in and conform.

You love being around people, but until you know someone well, you do not open up or share anything of consequence. You can be so charming that people don't realize you've been keeping them at bay with pleasant, light, safe conversation. It is understandable because once trust is broken or you are hurt, it is hard for you to move on. You have a substantial sense of personal pride and dignity that you guard. You are a great protector, so if someone you care about is harmed, you will do all you can to remedy the situation. You do have to be careful that you do not criticize yourself or others too harshly. Your insights give your words more sharpness than you may know.

A Cancer Moon, like all the water Moons, gives the aura a magnetic pull that wants to merge with whatever is nearby. Imagine two drops of water growing closer until they barely touch and how they pull together to become one larger drop. The aura of a person with a Cancer Moon is more likely to absorb the patterns and energies it touches. This matters even when doing solo workings or divination. The last spell, reading, or ritual you did can get stuck in your head like a song on repeat, so cleanse thoroughly. This combination usually comes with a gift for house blessings, house wards, conducting rites of passage, and lunar magick.

Moon in Leo

Fiery Leo excites and enlivens your Libra air. You know you are a star, and you are just looking for the right time and place to shine. Stop looking and shine wherever you are now, and the rest will follow. You are called to leadership and trendsetting more than most Libras. Be clear on your role, image, and desired outcomes, and you'll stay on track. Your ideals are central to how you live your life. You aim for larger than life, and the story you tell can excite and enliven other people. You have much to say and you take up a lot of space, which can lead to conflicts when you stop listening. Lean in to your Libra Sun and remember that leadership is a dialogue. Even when you are not officially in charge, you have a powerful influence.

You are fiercely independent and see rules as suggestions to be followed when they suit you. This combination tends to be highly romantic and idealistic, typically about people, but for some, this energy is directed to arts, media, or causes. There is a devotional undertone to almost everything in your life. Those who are close to you need to be able to reel you in when you are burning a bit too brightly. You don't know when to stop whether it is work or play. Your friends and loved ones need to be secure in their self-worth so that they can truly be your peers. You have too many goals to accomplish well in a lifetime, and you want excellence. Actively ask the universe for clues and guidance rather than using trial and error and educated guesses on what to pursue and what to shelve.

A Leo Moon, like all the fire element Moons, easily stretches forth to connect with the energy of other beings, though a little bit less than Aries and Sagittarius. The fiery qualities act to cleanse and protect your aura from picking up other people's emotional debris or being influenced by your environment. It is relatively easy for you to blend your energy with others and to separate cleanly. The Leo Moon also makes it easier for you to find your center and stay centered. Your magick is well suited to cleansings, healing, love, and glamour. You also can act as a catalyst that awakens magick in the people around you when you reach out your energy.

Moon in Virgo

The earthiness of Virgo makes you more organized and disciplined. This blend makes you more detail focused, methodical, and task oriented. You make plans and you get them done brilliantly. You have an air of casual sophistication that tends to put most people at ease. Your very beneficial and accurate words may land like sharp criticism. You can use your command of language and your gut instincts to reframe or redirect their response so that it ends up being productive. You are invested in helping people live productive and healthy lives. You are resistant to sharing truly personal information though you are good at giving the impression of being an open book. This may be good in formal or business settings but is problematic for letting people get close to you.

Compassion for yourself is necessary for your physical and mental health. You have a tendency to overthink and get caught in worrying loops. Health and healthy practices need to be important topics for you. Remind yourself that your Libra Sun wants harmony, beauty, and balance and that your Virgo Moon demands perfection in even the smallest details. This can be the impetus for greatness but can often result in irritation and disappointment. Being human is not a sign of inadequacy. Moreover, you can't control everything no matter how hard you try. You are more self-sufficient than most Libras, but you still need people you know are on your team. Make sure that the look and feel of your home and work environment are as soothing as possible. This has an impact on your health and happiness.

A Virgo Moon, like all the earth element Moons, generates an aura that is magnetic and pulls energy inward. This Moon also makes it easier to create strong thoughtforms and energy constructs. You have strong shields, but if breached, your shields tend to hang on to the pattern of injury; get some healing help, or the recovery may take longer than it should. Spells and workings related to oaths, promises, bindings, and agreements are assisted by this Moon. You can develop a gift for financial and business magick.

♎

Moon in Libra

Living well and fully as a double Libra requires you to learn to see the world as it is. If you recognize that the best you can do is tend to your tasks and not take on other people's work, you will be fine. You are good at attracting powerful friends and allies because people can feel your optimism and love of harmony. This grace does have a downside in that you sometimes walk away from opportunities that will be challenging and require some conflict. You love the power of fantasy and the imagination, and going inward can be a great resting place, but you will fade if you stay there. Your Libra nature needs contact with people and places to remain vital and flourishing. You are a social creature, and it doesn't matter if you are an extrovert, an introvert, or an ambivert, you need time with people to stay healthy.

Although you are caring and accommodating to your friends and partners, you will not tolerate being ignored, underappreciated, or put upon. Keep looking until you find the right people. Make more time in your life for your spiritual and magickal endeavors, as these activities truly feed your soul. You are tolerant and open-minded about most things so long as your happiness, and that of your beloveds, is not at risk. Pick which battles you'll take on and which are a waste of your well-chosen words. You are good at spotting trends in pop culture, society, business, and pretty much anything related to groups of people. This could be just fodder for conversation or part of your livelihood. You are inherently a member of many communities because you are a complex blend of identities. This can be a great benefit to you if used with awareness and finesse.

A Libra Moon, like all the air Moons, makes it easier to engage in soul travel and psychism and gives the aura greater flexibility. When you are working well with your Libra Moon, you can make yourself a neutral and clear channel for information from spirits and other entities. You are also able to tune in to unspoken requests when doing divinatory work. This Moon also helps you do work for sweetening sour situations, making peace, healing emotions, and encouraging personal development. Venus is Libra's ruling planet, so you also have a gift for the magick of love, beauty, self-worth, and the release of old sorrows.

Moon in Scorpio

A Scorpio Moon pours a tremendous amount of emotion into your Libra mind. As a Libra, you are always evaluating your environment, and the Scorpio Moon makes you investigate deeper and sharper. You also have more passions, drives, and internal storms than most Libras. You also pick up on other people's emotions, which is a gift and a challenge. Unlike most Libras, you are more willing to engage in direct conflict. You have a sharp wit and pride yourself on your piercing intelligence. Your enthusiasm can override your sense of diplomacy at times. Scorpio Moon gives you more determination, and that means when you commit, you are all in. Like most Libras, you seem easygoing, but when needed, you are unflinching, audacious, and formidable.

When you take an interest in someone, you can be remarkably intense. Try to ramp up slowly so you don't scare people off. This Sun and Moon blend also makes it easier to notice the darkness and turbulence within yourself and in the world. You can swing between being overly proud and your own worst critic. The middle between these two is the personal truth you are looking for. You can stop the cycle by assessing things from scratch with as much detachment as you can muster. You are creative and enterprising, but some help on following through and sticking with your plans and deadlines is needed. Scorpio Moon gives you an air of mystery and sensual magnetism.

You do love your secrets, and other people love to give you their secrets; this is a sacred trust. How well you keep them is how well you will feel about yourself. You are not immune to envy or jealousy, and both are dangerous for you.

A Scorpio Moon, like all the water Moons, gives the aura a magnetic pull that wants to merge with whatever is nearby. You easily absorb information about other people, spirits, places, and so on. Your path for purification is to feel things fully so you can fully release them. Your words or thoughts can turn into magick when you are emotional, so be careful. You have a gift for sigil work, creating altars and shrines, and writing and performing incantations and invocations. Mediumship is an option for you, but you need to have spirit guides or human warders while you do the work so that you feel comfortable enough to go deeper.

Moon in Sagittarius

You are always on the go mentally or physically and looking for adventure. You have enough interests to keep you busy for several lifetimes. You are a jack-of-all-trades and a master of some, though how many you master will be set by how much self-discipline you acquire. If something is romantic, otherworldly, foreign, or odd, it has your full interest. You tend toward optimism and seeing the glass as half full. However, when things are truly a mess, you will tell your story as if it were an epic saga where good triumphs in the end. You are good at looking at all the available information and making predictions that border on the prophetic when it involves the big picture. You are not as good at guessing the same for individuals.

Your exuberance and inspiration often put you in the spotlight. Like most Libras, you do not look for fights, but your habit of honesty bordering on rudeness can bring you woe. Be attentive and thoughtful of what you say and what you say you'll do. Your reputation is often shaped by what you've said in a moment of passion. When it doesn't work out, remember that you have humor and a silver-tongue on your side. In the end, even your adversaries are likely to admit you have admirable traits. You are affectionate, playful, and often romantic, but you need lots of space and freedom in your relationships. You also have a bit of a competitive streak in your temperament. You enjoy traveling, and going on a trip with someone is a good way to gauge long-term compatibility.

The auras of people with Sagittarius Moon are the most adaptable of the fire Moons. Your energy can reach far and change its shape easily. You are particularly good at affecting other people's energy or the energy of a place. Like the other fire Moons, your aura is good at cleansing itself, but it is not automatic and requires your conscious choice. This is because the mutable fire of Sagittarius is changeable and can go from a small ember to a pillar of fire that reaches the sky. You may have a favorite type or style of witchcraft or magick, but you are a generalist at heart. You can fit into a wide range of traditions and rituals so well that you may be mistaken for being a member when you are a guest. You have a gift for magick to heal places, both natural and human made.

♑
Moon in Capricorn

You are a bit colder and more reserved than most Libras. The Capricorn Moon makes you more competitive and power seeking. Your Libra Sun is ambivalent about your strong need to succeed. It is not reasonable or possible to be good at everything, so don't feel bad when you aren't the best. It is praiseworthy that you have high standards and try to reach them. That really is enough. You are really good at managing people and conversations. There is something political in almost everything you say or do. By *political*, I mean your actions are intended to influence people's perspectives and actions. To some people, it may look like you are socializing, but you are always working to nudge things in the direction of your plans. You need to feel financially safe to avoid distress; this is one of your strongest motivators.

Your communication skills and sense of purpose make you influential. You didn't have the easiest of childhoods, but it gave you strength and powerful lessons. That is all the motivation you need to do what you can to make things better. Your principles and the people you trust will keep you grounded and connected to your hopes. Ego can be an issue with this Sun and Moon combination. There is a tendency to think too highly of yourself, and then events bring about the reverse, and you think too little of yourself. Take stock of the facts and assess who you are and who you want to be so you can plan but not judge. You like to think that you're a loner, but you are not. Don't be stubborn and allow yourself to be open to your feelings. In love and friendship, you are caring, reliable, and encouraging. Just make sure your needs get met too.

A Capricorn Moon, like all the earth element Moons, generates an aura that is magnetic and pulls energy inward. What you draw to yourself tends to stick and solidify, so be wary, especially when doing healing work or cleansings. Call on the air of your Libra Sun to keep things flexible. The magick of a Capricorn Moon is excellent at imposing a pattern or creating a container in a working. Your spells and workings tend to be durable. You have a talent for luck charms, protective magick, banishings, and curse-breaking. Time-walking—spiritual time travel—is something you may want to try.

≈≈

Moon in Aquarius

With both your Sun and Moon in air signs, you'd think they'd blend easily, but they don't. You are avant-garde, experimental, and like to live in the moment. You are highly original and resilient against attempts to make you fall in line. You don't see a need to follow norms unless you see a reason that appeals to you. If you are pushed, you become rebellious. This unique approach to life also extends to your sense of what friendships and relationships should be. Loyalty and connection matter to you, but the need for options and change have equal say in your choices. Though generally you keep things on an even keel, when you lose your balance, you become volatile. You can be compassionate, crochety, welcoming, unduly cheerful, and unyielding all in the same hour. This is a sign that self-care is warranted. Lose yourself for a time in books, music, movies, and so on.

This combination lets you see many different angles and perspectives at once, so you will often notice details and trends others miss. You might be just a step ahead in time than others. Make use of the opportunities that information creates. Knowing is good, but doing is better. You spend so much time observing others and your surroundings that you neglect examining yourself. Although you are tolerant and broad-minded as a general rule and sociable, you tend to only become close to people who share a good portion of your core values. Take your time and learn from each relationship as you go. You are enchanting, the world is large, so you need not fret about being alone, but bide your time and choose well. You have a gift for creating graceful cooperation between people—in an organization, working on a project, in a social group, and so on. This will be one of the keys to your success.

Like all the air Moons, the Aquarius Moon encourages a highly mobile and flexible aura. You have an air Moon, so grounding is important, but focusing on your core and center is more important. From that center, you can strengthen and stabilize your power. People with Aquarius Moon are good at shaping and holding a specific thoughtform or energy pattern and transferring it to other people or into objects. You have skill in divination for groups, whether that be covens, businesses, nations, or circumstances that affect many. There is also a gift for enchanting objects and perhaps for bringing out latent talents in others.

Moon in Pisces

Libra is mostly concerned with one-on-one relationships, but a Pisces Moon expands this desire to connect in a more universal way. You feel compassion and make every effort to offer kindness and consideration to a broad range of people because you feel the weight of the world. This blend does give you great sensitivity, intuition, psychism, and the words and images to describe what you receive. In your day-to-day life, you are closer to your psychism and the other worlds than most Libras. You are good at spotting deception, understanding undercurrents in events around you, but with a weakness. You can be fooled by those who offer you friendship or love. Although it is generally admirable to look for the best in people, it is also wise to use your intellect and intuition to see the whole truth.

Your imagination and creativity will open the way for many career options. This doesn't necessarily mean you will be in the arts, but it does mean that your originality will be the key to success. For example, you can always come up with several ways to describe or explain something, which is useful in teaching, negotiating, and so on. You give off a welcoming air and have an endearing sense of humor and whimsy that will help both your work and your home life. Do be careful lest your imagination lead to fantasies that keep you from living in the here and now. You must choose to keep grounded and anchored, or you'll make poor choices based on impressions and hopes rather than facts. Many of your doubts and bouts of indecision will lessen as you understand yourself and your aspirations. You will also become more authentic and let others know what you truly feel and think.

With a Pisces Moon, the emphasis should be on learning to feel and control the rhythm of your energetic motion in your aura. Pisces Moon is the most likely to pick up and hang on to unwanted emotions or energies. Rippling your energy and bouncing things off the outer layers of your aura is a good defense. Be careful, develop good shielding practices, and make cleansing yourself and your home a regular practice. Practices that involve going into trance come easily for you, but make sure you have a helper. Your storytelling is a form of magick as well, and you may wish to write visualizations and pathworkings. Dreamwork is also one of your strong suits.

TAROT
CORRESPONDENCES
Ivo Dominguez, Jr.

♎

You can use the tarot cards in your work as a Libra witch for more than divination. They can be used as focal points in meditations and trance to connect with the power of your sign or element or to understand it more fully. They are great on your altar as an anchor for the powers you are calling. You can use the Minor Arcana cards to tap into Moon, Saturn, or Jupiter in Libra energy even when they are in other signs in the heavens. If you take a picture of a card, shrink the image and print it out; you can fold it up and place it in spell bags or jars as an ingredient.

Libra Major Arcana

Justice

All the Air Signs

Ace of Swords

Libra Minor Arcana

2 of Swords	Moon in Libra
3 of Swords	Saturn in Libra
4 of Swords	Jupiter in Libra

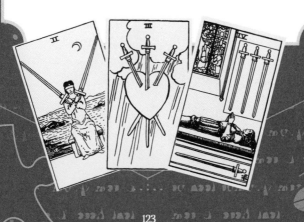

Patti Wigington

While none of us really like to stereotype ourselves, I've had plenty of *wooo I'm SUCH a Libra right now* moments. For better or worse, they often manifest during times when I'm focused on something spiritual, such as ritual or spell work, working with my coven, or even attending events such as festivals or workshops. Although I've learned over the years to be wary of specific Libra pitfalls and traps, it does require a bit of mindfulness to keep myself focused.

The Justice Spell That Worked Too Well

One of the things I always caution new practitioners about is the importance of *really* thinking about what your intention is before you even begin crafting a spell. Why? Well, because if it works properly, you're going to get exactly what you ordered ... and sometimes that's not what you actually want. It's that old chestnut about being careful what you wish for.

And it's a lesson I learned the hard way, with the very first spell I actually cast.

Way back when, in the days when I was too young to know any better, I decided that a recent speeding ticket would be the target of my witchy wisdom. I had been on a road trip, visiting friends in Ohio, and was on my way back to my home in South Carolina. Somewhere in the mountains, just outside Beckley, West Virginia, as I flew along the highway with my windows down and Van Halen cranked up to eleven on the stereo, I heard a *bloop-BLOOOP*, and looked in my rearview mirror to see red lights flashing from the top of a state trooper's car. I did what most people would do—I panicked, and then I pulled over.

The officer, who looked like everything you'd imagine a stereotypical 1980s trooper would look like, strolled up nonchalantly and asked if I knew how fast I'd been going. I did, but I wasn't going to admit it, so I simply said, "No sir, but I bet you're about to tell me."

Now, I have to be honest and fair to Officer Whatsisname. I was driving *waaaay* over the speed limit, and he was completely justified in handing me a nice blue piece of paper with all the details on it, including the address for the courthouse where I could mail a check for 164 dollars to pay my fine (this was long before we could pay tickets online).

I totally deserved to get popped for speeding; I own that, 100 percent.

Here's my Libra moment.

We Libras are all about justice, right? Well, by the time I finished my drive and got back to South Carolina, I was indignant. I was offended. I had, somewhere between Beckley and home, managed to convince myself that I had been somehow *wronged* by Officer Whatsisname. I got it in my head that this whole speeding ticket situation was just plain *unfair*. So, I decided that in order to make this 164-dollar problem go away, I would turn to the recently discovered world of magic. I was nineteen, cocky, and didn't really understand diddly-squat about spell work, but by golly, I was gonna witchcraft this ticket right out of existence.

Famous last words.

Because, my friends, I was a clueless newbie Libra witch who cast an absolutely magnificent spell calling *for truth and justice to prevail*.

Yeah. You read that right. As I'm sure you can imagine, this did not go quite as I expected.

Let truth and justice prevail! I said, waving hands mystically under a full Moon.

Boy, did it ever. The fine was due within fourteen days, and I opted not to pay it—because magic, right? Well, thirty days later, I got a letter from the Bureau of Motor Vehicles, cheerfully letting me know my driver's license was temporarily suspended because of my failure to pay a fine in West Virginia. That was followed by a letter from my insurance company, telling me they had canceled my policy for the same reason. As if that wasn't bad enough, I also got slapped with two bills for other stuff I had legitimately forgotten to pay. By the time I got my act together, paid the traffic ticket, restored my suspended driver's license, gotten my insurance policy back in line, and paid off the defaulted bills, this 164-dollar ticket (that I never wanted to pay in the first place, despite it being completely justified) cost me *close to 700 dollars*.

After that experience, I took a lot of time for self-reflection. Maybe magic and witchcraft wasn't for me after all—clearly, it had bitten me right in the butt! But then I realized a couple of things had happened. First of all, the spell *had* worked. It did exactly what I called it to do, so technically I was batting with a 100 percent success rate. It's just that I didn't put enough thought into what I was casting for—truth and justice did indeed prevail, in more ways than I had ever anticipated or wanted.

Second, I learned that there's a big difference between what is actually fair or just, versus what we want to happen. I *wanted* to not have to shell out 164 dollars to the state of West Virginia. But what was just and fair was for me to acknowledge my Speed Racer behavior on the highway and pay what I owed.

Finally, it occurred to me—again, after a great deal of self-reflection—that rather than just blindly working up a spell when I was emotional and mad, I'd have been far better off listening to my natural Libra instincts. Had I taken the time to evaluate what I was about to do and weigh some different options, I'd have probably skipped casting this spell altogether, or maybe done one on myself to make me a more responsible driver. Now, when I begin crafting a spell or working of any kind, I work my way through a mental flowchart, using an if-then approach. If I call for X, and the spell is effective, then the result will be Y. I learned, painfully, from this experience that an impulsive Libra can be a dangerous one—because I wasn't clear enough on my intentions, I ended up being my own target.

Years later—and I mean, a good decade and a half after this happened, when I had gotten more responsible with my magic (as well as my driving)—I found myself considering another justice-related spell. And this time, I put some serious thought into it to make sure my wording actually matched my intentions.

The Magical Speed Bump

I lived with my family—including my spouse, my nine-year-old daughter, and toddler twins—on a nice little one-way street in a quiet neighborhood. It was the kind of neighborhood where everyone knew the people on their street, we all spent a lot of time visiting each other's front porches, and kids ran pretty much nonstop between one house and the next. However, because my street was the connector between a large public park and a main artery, we sometimes saw cars going the wrong way; it didn't happen often, and usually if we shouted and waved, drivers realized their mistake, turned around apologetically, and went back the way they came.

Unfortunately, there was a local teen who not only went the wrong way regularly, but he did it at speeds far too high for a neighborhood full of kids. I had called the police about it a couple of times, but they really couldn't help unless they saw it happen.

So (wait for it) I decided to make some magic. This time, I was very deliberate about my working. I didn't want anyone getting hurt, and I wasn't stupid enough to do my truth and justice spell from years gone by—I just wanted this kid to stay off my street. In fact, what I specifically called for was him getting pulled over by the police, inspiring him toward better behavior behind the wheel.

The spell involved a Matchbox car, a length of track, and little gravel piles arranged into speedbumps—and at the end of the street was a mirror and a small set of scales. Justice personified. About ten days later, the neighborhood hotshot came zipping down the street at top speed, traveling the wrong way as always, and suddenly slammed on his brakes. His car came to rest wedged up against a wooden utility pole, knocking it over in the process; clearly, he wasn't injured because he backed up, turned around, and raced off. One of my neighbors called the police to report the damaged pole.

When the officer arrived, he discovered a license plate embedded in the wooden pole. He took a report, ran the tag, and said he'd go pay a visit to Speedy McSpeederpants. He must have done so—while I don't know if there was any sort of legal action that took place, what I do know is no one ever saw that car go flying up our street the wrong way again, and I didn't have to worry anymore about him running over any of the kids in my neighborhood.

This time around, I used what I'd learned from my earlier mistake. I put thought into the process, used my words wisely, and ended up solving a problem in a way that didn't turn around and cost me.

Learning to use your natural Libra skills in a way that's thoughtful and balanced: priceless.

YOUR RISING SIGN'S INFLUENCE

Ivo Dominguez, Jr.

The rising sign, also known as the ascendant, is the sign that was rising on the eastern horizon at the time and place of your birth. In the birth chart, it is on the left side on the horizontal line that divides the upper and lower halves of the chart. Your rising sign is also the cusp of your first house. It is often said that the rising sign is the mask you wear to the world, but it is much more than that. It is also the portal through which you experience the world. The sign of your ascendant colors and filters those experiences. Additionally, when people first meet you, they meet your rising sign. This means they interact with you based on their perception of that sign rather than your Sun sign. This in turn has an impact on you and how you view yourself. As they get to know you over time, they'll meet you as your Sun sign. Your ascendant is like the colorful clouds that hide the Sun at dawn, and as the Sun continues to rise, it is revealed.

The rising sign also has an influence on your physical appearance as well as your style of dress. To some degree, your voice, mannerisms, facial expressions, stance, and gait are also swayed by the sign of your ascendant. The building blocks of your public persona come from your rising sign. How you arrange those building blocks is guided by your Sun sign, but your Sun sign must work with what it has been given. For witches, the rising sign shows some of the qualities and foundations for the magickal personality you can construct. The magickal personality is much more than simply shifting into the right headspace, collecting ritual gear, lighting candles, and so on. The magickal persona is a construct that is developed through your magickal and spiritual practices to serve as an interface between different parts of the self. The magickal persona, also known as the magickal personality, can also act as a container or boundary so that the mundane and the magickal parts of a person's life can each have its own space. Your rising also gives clues about which magickal techniques will come naturally to you.

This chapter describes the twelve possible arrangements of rising signs with a Libra Sun and what each combination produces. There are 144 possible kinds of Libras when you take into consideration the Moon signs and rising signs. You may wish to reread the chapter on your Moon sign after reading about your rising sign so you can better understand these influences when they are merged.

Aries Rising

Your desire to do everything and go everywhere is sped up and stimulated by the Aries rising. You never lose the ability to get excited, enthused, and passionate the way a teenager can. You love being playful, and a hint of competition makes everything more interesting. You love making an impression, so you often become a center of attention. Your exterior is very outgoing and bold, but your inner self is much less confident, so you are always wondering how you get yourself into so many predicaments. Most people with this combination benefit from physical practices that are well structured and become a routine. It doesn't matter whether it is yoga, tai chi, dance—so long as you do it. This consumes excess energy so you can concentrate and reduces your stress.

Having the ruling planets of Venus and Mars active in your chart means you will exude power, poise, and sensuality. Be advised that not everyone understands your verbal sparring and physical humor are meant as harmless fun or sometimes flirting. This combo loves a good debate, and you are competitive and relentless. You would make a good lawyer, advocate, community organizer, and so on. You are definitely more aggressive than most other Libras and swing back and forth between fierce and placid. You are also quicker to jump into relationships, contracts, and so on. Let your Libra Sun look things over first.

An Aries rising means that when you reach out to draw in power, both air and fire will answer easily. If you need other types of energy, you need to reach farther, focus harder, and be more specific in your request. This combination often attracts the attention of the spirits, Fae, and other beings, so be mindful of what you say aloud. You excel at spells for strength, confidence, or removing obstacles. These can be cast for yourself or others.

Taurus Rising

You get a double dose of Venus rulership with this rising. You also are more likely to slow down enough to smell the roses and enjoy all the sensual delights of life. Warmhearted, sensual, stylish, amorous, and sweet don't even begin to describe your allure. You love peace and mutual respect and strive to bring that bliss into the world. You will speak when you have run through the possibilities and are ready to stick with your statement. You don't like arguments or conflict and if there is too much noise and emotional turmoil, you become distracted or obstinate. It is better that you leave until things cool down rather than becoming more embroiled.

A Taurus rising encourages you to be trustworthy, practical, circumspect, and frugal. This combination asks your Libra energy to behave in ways that yield longer-lasting results. This combination does make you more likely to show the common Libra trait of giving away too much of your independence for the sake of peace and quiet. If you begin to slow down and are less productive, it is a sign you are not being fair to yourself and are running low on the juice of life. Rising signs change how you perceive things, and, combined with your Libra Sun, this blend allows you to see the way through the twists and turns of the labyrinth of society and diplomacy.

Taurus rising gives more strength in your aura and the capacity to maintain a more solid shape to your energy. This gives you stronger shields and allows you to create thoughtforms and spells that are longer lasting. This combination also makes you a better channel for other people's energy in group work because you can tolerate larger volumes of different types of energies. You can act as an amplifier to boost individuals or small groups to increase their magickal or psychic abilities.

♊
Gemini Rising

Double the air and Mercury ruling your rising make you sparkle in social settings. You don't even need to turn on the charm to be noticed. You often get your way through gentle persuasion. You are always looking for new experiences, fresh conversation, new music, and styles that express your mood. You move easily between different age-groups, backgrounds, cultures, and so on. Learn to breathe deep and listen more than you speak. You'll miss out on less when you do so. You do need to guard against taking life a little too easily and not challenging yourself to do more. You have a considerable amount of raw talent for a variety of activities, but it requires choices and actions to convert potential to actuality. Fear of missing out is best addressed by prioritizing your life choices and engaging in life.

Generally, you are a positive person, but if you are blocked from communicating your ideas for too long, your frustration may go past anger and into an unfeeling state. Before you get this blocked up, backtrack, make new plans, use that amazing imagination to find a way around the situation. Ask for help; you'll get all you need. In work settings, learn to say no more often as you already have too many tasks to manage. In your personal relationships, learn to speak more fully and authentically about your feelings. Your desire not to ruffle feathers will lead to larger issues in the long run.

This rising helps your energy and aura stretch farther and adapt to whatever it touches. This combination can lend itself to communication with animals, plants, crystals, and anything with a spirit. You can pick up too much information, and it can be overwhelming. Learn to narrow down and control your awareness of other people's thoughts and feelings. You have a gift that can help or hinder technology and can impact the digital realm.

Cancer Rising

Cancer rising makes you a bit more of a homebody and a bit more reserved. Like most Libras, you are observant of other people's feelings and behaviors, but Cancer rising gives you more insight into their motivations. You can often describe what a person is feeling or wanting better than they can. This sensitivity can be brought to bear in work as a teacher, counselor, translator, negotiator, and so on. There are many other ways you can use this skill. You have a stronger need for reassurance than most Libras. Try to remain neutral and don't jump to conclusions about how others feel about you. More often than not, the situations being discussed are not about you.

Cancer rising with a Libra Sun tends to come with a strong sense of aesthetics, especially in decor and gardens. Cancer also gives you a love of the past and history and a touch of sentimentality. There is also a pull to be more nurturing and to preserve living beings and material goods that have emotional value and memories attached to them. You tend to be drawn more to the generations before or after yours. The people close to you should be orderly, calm, and well grounded. Your great gift is sensitivity, but you need safe and quiet places for rest and refuge. Music is one of the best restoratives for you.

Cancer rising grants the power to use your emotions, or the emotional energy of others, to power your witchcraft. Though you can draw on a wide range of energies to fuel your magick, raising power through emotion is the simplest method. This rising produces ease and power in Moon magick of any sort. You are also good at charging oils, waters, and other liquids. You may have a calling for dreamwork, past-life recall, and house blessings.

Leo Rising

Leo is ruled by the Sun, so you move through the world with a spotlight on you and some theme music in the background. You are articulate and can come up with the right language to catch hearts and minds. You aim for compassion and honorable behavior in all areas of your life. Leo is firmer in its stance than Libra, which can help you stand up for yourself and make demands. You have a great deal of self-confidence; however, the downside is that, when thwarted, Leo rising mixed with those Libra winds can get very stormy. You regret your outburst almost immediately but console yourself with the fact that it was probably needed.

This blend loves the good things in life, so don't forget to attend to your career needs. You are good at guiding people to do better, and this is best done by leading by example. You are fearless in most situations, except when you find out that you made an error or had the wrong information. The more you learn to let go of the agitation this provokes, the smoother your life will be. Unlike most Libras, you can give the impression of being too interested in yourself. Make sure the people near you know that you see them and appreciate them. Drink plenty of water every day because this air and fire combo needs a large amount of water to cool and cleanse you.

Leo rising means that when you reach out to draw in power, fire will answer first. If you need other types of energy, you need to reach farther, focus harder, and be more specific in your request. Your aura and energy are brighter and steadier than most people's, so you attract the attention of spirits, deities, and so on. Your Sun and rising give you an aptitude for energy healing, weather work, and ritual theater. You also can control the emotional and spiritual atmosphere of a room with ease.

Virgo Rising

Virgo and Libra both know details matter, but Virgo is focused on the process and Libra on the outcomes of the process. Libra's social skills and Virgo's attention to detail and careful analysis can be wonderful or frightful. You are sharp and incisive in your understanding of most matters, and the Virgo gives you reserve and control to hold back. Don't underestimate the impact of your words and opinions. You have a strong calling to be of service, to work for a healthier world. In your eagerness, you may neglect getting enough rest and recreation. You are prone to wanting perfection in all things and may expect too much of yourself and others. Don't turn your friends or coworkers into improvement projects, as nobody will be happy.

You are shyer and pickier than most Libras when it comes to friends and partners. You also seem a bit less approachable than most Libras. You do have the Libra skill of conversation and interaction, so opening your mind to connect with others is easy. It must be someone special to open your heart and keep it open. You have high standards and expectations for people close to you. You have so much mental activity that you need to schedule time to cool down your nervous system. Please make use of meditation, discussion groups, or therapists.

This blend makes it easier to work with divinities who are connected to the element of air, wisdom, communication, and healing. You are good at spells to let go of patterns and habits that do not serve you. You are a good diagnostician who can figure out what is wrong with a ritual, what is preventing a healthy flow of energy in a person or home, and so on. Be careful when you entwine your energy with someone else because you can pick up and retain their patterns and issues. Always cleanse your energy after doing solo or collective work.

♎

Libra Rising

Double Libra gives you a glow that is felt as much as it is seen. When you step into the room, everything tries to harmonize with you. There is something in your aura that is like a fragrance, music, or a familiar feeling that makes people open up to you and be inclined to like you. Use your power to fascinate others with kindness. You can also change to match your environment and become not invisible but at one with it. If you are honest with yourself, you prefer to be a rolling stone than a cornerstone. You get things started and when things seem stable enough you want to move on. You prefer to be on the move and have a variety of experiences.

Try to work on time management because being late or missing deadlines is something that will eventually cause serious issues. You want to take time to see all the possibilities, but create firm time allotments for your tasks. Also, for your sake and the sake of the people you actually want to spend time with, say no more often, redraw, and reinforce your boundaries. Don't forget to read the fine print in written agreements, the subtext in conversations, and pay attention to your intuition. Your Libra rising wants you to be fair and treat everyone equally; this is not true for some people. Be mindful of endocrine issues as balance in your body is the key to health.

When you expand your aura, your personal energy can settle down an unruly or unwholesome atmosphere or calm down irritated spirits. Magick related to bringing peace or justice is favored by this combination. Rituals or spells to mend friendships and relationships or improve communication are favored. This combination also works well in creating crystal grids, working altars, magickal gardens, or other physical instances of beauty and magick.

Scorpio Rising

There is tension between your rising sign and your Sun, which can be productive and energizing or create strain and distress. You must actively maintain a balance between pessimism and optimism. You are not darker than most Libras, you are just more aware of your dark side. You scrutinize, you dig, and you dispel illusions with your piercing intellect. Your thought process is complicated, layered, and woven through with many strands of emotion. Though you are creative, you tend more toward investigation, research, or specialties that make the most of your probing mind. You are a little less talkative than most Libras, but when you do speak, it is full of meaning and implications.

To be loved and to be loved in return is a goal you hold in secret. You radiate sensuality, which can be a problem or a gift. This rising is cautious about sharing their deep self, so humor, snark, and hot takes will be used to hold others at arm's length. Remind yourself that we all make mistakes and choose forgiveness when it is possible and reasonable. Sometimes, the best option is time and distance. Scorpio rising can make you more reactive to drugs, toxins, and allergens, so be careful. That said, you have significant regenerative powers and can overcome most physical ills.

Scorpio rising makes your energy capable of pushing through most energetic barriers. You can dissolve illusion or bring down wards or shields and see through to the truth. You may have an aptitude for breaking curses and lifting oppressive spiritual atmospheres. It is important that you do regular cleansing work for yourself. You are likely to end up doing messy work and you do not have a nonstick aura. You are a natural in rituals or workings to explore past lives, call the dead, or reveal hidden truths. Be cautious when making pledges, oaths, or promises in rituals.

Sagittarius Rising

Sagittarius loves understanding, the big picture, optimism, and ambitious plans that expand the interests of a Libra Sun. You value direct speech, which means your bluntness can get you into predicaments, but you often smooth things over with your positive intentions. You are often surprised by the effect that your statements have on people. You are constantly looking to improve yourself, but the first thing you need is more follow-through and sticking to your plans. Your criticism of yourself and others tends to be constructive rather than destructive.

You are more boisterous and outgoing than most Libras. Sagittarius loves freedom and expressing their opinions. Libra wants to find the best arrangement and most harmonious placements for all the people and things in their life. It is easy to see the good situations and the dilemmas that arise from this combination. You can confuse the people close to you because you are caring and affectionate, but when you are in the midst of a project or exploring something interesting, you seem to forget they exist. Physical activity, whether it is sports, dancing, hiking, or whatever you can manage, is essential to your quality of life. This combo lets you appreciate and enjoy food and drink, sometimes to excess.

Sagittarius rising adds mutable fire to your cardinal air so your aura changes shape at will. Talent in the use of candles, wands, or staves is favored by this combination. This is because you can push your energy and intentions into objects with ease. You have a talent for rituals and spells that call forth creativity, wisdom, and freedom. You attract the attention of spirits and divine beings easily. You can be a voice for them if you wish. This combination gives access to lots of energy, but you can fry yourself with the intensity of the current. Make it your practice to stop and cool off and then start again.

Capricorn Rising

When people first meet you, it may be some time until they see your Libra nature. You are not as sociable, are more serious, restless, and forceful in achieving whatever you want. You give the impression of being more conservative and reserved than you really are. You tend to be harder on yourself than on other people. Since you are goal oriented, remind yourself that you can't do better unless you see your own progress and potential. You are a strong advocate, supporter, and sometimes defender of the people in your life. Both your Sun and rising are in cardinal signs, so you must strive to handle that drive and ambition in a healthy way. You can handle your money and work life with great attention to detail. A good amount of your self-esteem is tied to your work in the world.

This combo produces a good blending of head and heart, which makes you reasonable and practical in your personal life. You have strong needs and expectations in all your relationships, so you need people who can hold their own. You also do best with people who value stability and loyalty. You are very aware of human fragilities in yourself and in others, so it is important to learn how to manage your expectations for perfect behavior. If you don't, you miss out on important people and opportunities.

Capricorn rising creates an aura and energy field that are slow to come up to speed, but have amazing momentum once fully activated. Make it your habit to do some sort of energy work or meditative warmup before engaging in witchcraft. Mandalas, mudras, and motion in general work well for you. Try working with crystals, stones, and even geographic features like mountains as your magick blends well with them. Your rituals and spells benefit from having a structure and a plan of action. Spells for removing obstacles, clear thinking, and business ventures are favored.

≈

Aquarius Rising

This rising brings a second dose of the element of air, which puts an emphasis on thought and the powers of the mind more so than communication. You buzz with an energy that others notice. For the most part, you are humanitarian and have a dozen plans, perspectives, and ideologies to make the world better. You like collective work and being on a team in theory, but you can find it hard to compromise. To make your ideas real, you must meet reality in the middle. Your offbeat humor and eccentric views will help you find a way. Your mental life is rich and interesting. Sometimes it is too interesting, and you forget to follow through on what you've promised individuals.

You like to be provocative and outrageous; sometimes this is for fun and sometimes it is to test others. Even when it looks random and spontaneous, you have planned out your actions. Caring about people arises from a mental and rational connection first that may, with time, become an emotional connection as well. You are not romantic in the normal sense of the word, but you do form strong bonds with people. You are affectionate but rarely emotionally needy. Those close to you need to be equally innovative or grounded and bighearted.

Your nervous system is high-strung and needs no additional strains upon it, so be kind to yourself and get some rest.

Aquarius rising helps make it easier for you to consciously change the shape and density of your aura. This makes you a generalist who can adapt to many styles and forms of magick. Witchcraft focused on calling inspiration, creating community, and personal transformation is supported by this combination. Aquarius rising is gifted at turning ideas into reality. Mind magick, psychism, weather magick, and energy work are good options for you. Working with colors and scents helps your workings.

Pisces Rising

This rising brings in more mutability, flowing emotions, and psychic perceptions. Most of the time, you are sensitive, tender, caring, and aware of others' needs. You are among the most loving and affectionate of all Libras. This combo may worsen the Libra predilection to being indecisive, so you must hone your will. Moreover, you need to accept that sometimes you need to cause someone else discomfort to follow your will. If you don't, then you can suffer from bouts of self-doubt and melancholy. Look to the people who are dependable and good-hearted in your life so they can give you good counsel and hold you accountable. Many people hold you in high regard, and you need to let them tell you how they see you.

You love to change, to experiment, with the look of your clothing, hair, and home. People look forward to seeing what you've done and if they'd like to try it. It is necessary for you to do wide-ranging searches and trial runs to find the jobs, friends, and partners who best match who you are. You are highly spiritual, and it is a little too easy to drift away and daydream. Stay grounded and present in the here and now or you won't bring your dreams to fruition. Getting good sleep is essential for your health. If you are not sleeping well, explore options to improve the quality of your sleep.

Pisces rising with your Libra Sun opens the gates of the imagination, the dreamworld, and the upperworld. You have a distinctive gift for helping others find their way to other levels of reality. You can do astral travel, hedge riding, and soul travel in all their forms with some training and practice. You have a gift for interpreting and understanding old magick and updating it so it can be used now. Music, poetry, chanting, and dance also provide fuel for your witchcraft.

A DISH FIT FOR A LIBRA: LEMON AND GINGER STIR-FRY FOR HARMONY

Dawn Aurora Hunt

* * *

This recipe brings together the sharpness of ginger and the pucker of lemon in a harmony to soothe the spirit as well as relationships.

The balance of flavors in this dish is perfect for you, Libra. With a little bite from complex and spicey ginger, and the soothing cleansing of lemon, this meal is perfect shared with a friend or on your own. Lemons are known for their purification powers, but also can bring about longevity in friendships. Ginger, on the other hand, is a powerful love and passion ingredient that lends itself to helping our bodies and minds digest what we take in. Using equal portions of red vegetables like tomatoes and bell peppers for love, protein like chicken or tofu for wellness, and quinoa for prosperity, this dish has visual and energic balance.

Omit chicken or use tofu to make this dish entirely vegan and use gluten-free soy sauce or tamari to make this recipe celiac friendly.

Ingredients:

+ 1 large red bell pepper, sliced
+ 1 large red onion, sliced
+ 1 cup sugar snap peas
+ 8 ounces broccoli florets
+ 8 ounces chicken thighs cut into bite-size pieces
+ 1 cup cornstarch
+ Salt and pepper to taste
+ 2 cups cooked quinoa (tricolor works well here)
+ Green onions (sliced) and golden sesame seeds for garnish

For the lemon-ginger sauce:

+ ½ cup vegetable broth or low-sodium chicken broth
+ 2 tablespoons soy sauce
+ 1 teaspoon toasted sesame oil
+ Juice from 2 fresh lemons
+ 1 tablespoon minced/grated fresh ginger
+ 6 cloves minced fresh garlic

- + 1 tablespoon honey
- + 2 tablespoons olive oil

Directions:

Make the sauce. In a small bowl, whisk together broth, soy sauce, sesame oil, lemon juice, ginger, garlic, and honey. Set aside.

Dredge chicken in cornstarch and season with salt and pepper if desired. Set aside.

In a large skillet, heat one tablespoon of olive oil on high heat. Sauté the vegetables about five minutes, until slightly cooked but still firm. Remove from the skillet. Heat remaining olive oil on high. Cook the chicken until lightly golden and cooked through, about five minutes. Lower the heat and add the vegetables back to the skillet. Pour on the lemon-ginger sauce and coat evenly. Cook on low heat an additional five minutes until sauce thickens slightly. Serve on top of cooked quinoa. Garnish with sliced green onions and golden sesame seeds if desired.

RECHARGING AND SELF-CARE

Patti Wigington

The life of a Libra witch can occasionally be exhausting. It's not uncommon for our emotional and spiritual equilibrium to get off-kilter, for a number of reasons. First of all, maintaining a constant quest for balance is *hard*. It takes work … and that can be tiring. As air signs, we Libras place a high value on logic and reason … but for better or worse, we're also very emotion driven. We try hard to be peacekeepers in our world, all the while being surrounded by chaos and disorder. It's a tough spot to be in sometimes!

Also, Libras tend to be the "therapy friend" because we're such good listeners; it's important to make sure we take care of ourselves in addition to being helpful and offering solutions and support to others. While Libras value relationships—and often put a *lot* of effort into maintaining them—we're also experts at mentally checking out of a situation when we feel like we just can't hang anymore. Make sure you allow yourself the gift of regular self-care, so you can recover, recharge, and rejuvenate.

Regular Self-Care Routines and Practices

Developing regular routines and practices for self-care can be a game changer for a Libra witch. Not only will you feel better on a holistic level as the mind, body, and spirit recover from challenges, but you'll have a more positive outlook and a fresh perspective about the world and all it has to offer. This, in turn, will give you the benefit of seeing your relationships with others in a whole new way, and being fully invested in them without draining yourself of your energy.

Take care of your soul and spirit. Learn to stay grounded and centered, forging a connection to stability and security. You can do this by starting your day with meditation or yoga, spending time alone when you're feeling overwhelmed, and learning to set appropriate boundaries for the people in your life. Remember, boundaries are how we train other people to treat us, but sticking to those boundaries is how we train our own spirit to be strong and empowered. Treat your physical body well, to the best of your ability. Libras usually enjoy a good power nap, and there's nothing wrong with that if you need it! It's also important to eat well and keep our bodies properly nourished; a healthy witch is often a happy witch. Be sure to work regular movement and physical activity into your routine as well if you're able. If you love exercise and it makes you feel good, make time for it. If you hate exercise and wouldn't be caught dead in a Pilates class, that's okay too—you can still get up and move around; go for walks, put on some music and dance around the living room, or take the stairs at work instead of the elevator.

Make time for meaningful connections. In this day and age, when we're often so isolated from others—or we're only connected to them virtually, via social media and texting—it's important to spend time, live and in person, with the people you care about the most. For the average Libra, it's about quality over quantity; if you'd rather avoid going to a concert with thousands of other music fans but prefer to sit on the porch and have a meal with three of your closest friends, do it. If you have a circle of pals who love the same luxuries as you—getting your hair or nails done, going out for ice cream, enjoying a weekend getaway, etc.—then take advantage of it and treat yourself to a good pampering session.

Learn to relax—even though it's sometimes tough. Libras have minds that are constantly on the go; we usually prefer being busy to being bored. One of the downsides of this is that it's often hard for us to just do *nothing*. Every once in a while, allow yourself the gift of a day where nothing is scheduled or planned. Want to spend the day in your pajamas on the couch, eating snacks and bingeing your favorite show? Feel like turning off your phone and ignoring your emails for an afternoon? Go for it! You'll be thankful you did.

Restore Your Connection to Power

Libras are pretty social animals—but we also need to disconnect once in a while and recharge our batteries, especially if we've been taking care of the needs of others. After all, you can't pour anything out of an empty cup. Taking a few simple steps can help boost your power levels back up, which will allow you to get back into the swing of things with a revitalized and positive outlook on life.

Make sure you're always challenging yourself—within reason. The Libra witch can easily get bored when life is stagnant, so change things up now and then. If work has become repetitive and dull, ask your boss for new responsibilities and projects. Is your love life predictable and routine? Invite your partner to try something new and exciting—take a class together, go for a spontaneous adventure, or spice up your bedroom activities with something out of your usual repertoire.

If you get restless, channel your energy into something new. Being restless can make us hostile toward others as well as to ourselves, creating a vicious cycle where we're just annoyed with everything and everyone. Rather than going with the flow and letting yourself feel dissatisfied, start a new creative endeavor, volunteer for a cause you're passionate about, or learn a skill you've always wanted to try.

Learn to deal with confrontation in a healthy way. Libras tend to be blunt—we can't help it, we're honest to a fault, but sometimes we get so caught up in our need for justice and fairness that we forget about tact. Plan your words in advance, so that when it's time to confront someone about uncomfortable subjects, you've got your talking points ready to go. It will save you from having to go apologize later. Thinking things through ahead of time is a great power booster, because it keeps us from feeling bad in the aftermath; think of it as emotional preventative maintenance.

Finally, give yourself a treat by taking a break now and then. It's perfectly fine—and healthy!—to tell other people you need space for a while. Use that period for personal growth, reflection, and self-development. Taking some time by yourself is vital to being able to reengage with others when you return to your social connections. By allowing yourself to reflect and recharge, you'll be more fully present in your relationships with others when you're ready to step back in.

Libra Wellness

In a society where we often see injustice and unfairness, Libras are especially vulnerable to feeling helpless or powerless about the world around us. Taking care of your mind, body, and spirit is crucial for the Libra witch; internal maintenance keeps us from becoming overwhelmed by all the external problems we see.

Libras enjoy their sleep—for us, our bed isn't just a place we lie down at the end of the day. It's so much more than that. It's our sanctuary. Bedtime for a Libra means allowing our brains to take a break from all the manic and creative things running through our heads, from solving the world's problems (and those of our friends, family, and random strangers who are drawn to us because they can tell we're good listeners), and from trying to achieve balance in a disharmonious world. One of the best things a Libra witch can do for themselves, in addition to getting a decent amount of sleep, is to turn the bedroom into a place that's cozy, welcoming, and comfortable. Treat yourself to the nice sheets and fluffy pillows, paint your bedroom walls a soothing color if you can, fill the space with art, books, and music, fragrances, or ambient sounds that calm and relax you.

The typical Libra also feels a strong connection to beauty and art. When you've had enough of the world at large, let yourself escape for a while to places that bring you joy. Find a local museum or gallery where you can wind down and surround yourself with things that are aesthetically pleasing. If you can't get to a place like this, why not make your own art? Turn off your phone, put on your favorite music, and create something of your own just to help your brain disengage.

Immerse yourself in the outdoors—it's good for us emotionally, physically, and spiritually. There's beauty and calm to be found in nature all around us—go for a hike in the woods, plant a garden, pick flowers in a field, or go to a local park and just *be* for a while. Lie in the grass, sit on a log, hug a tree, stick your toes in a stream. Nature helps us restore our inner sense of harmony. If you don't live in an area with a lot of green space, see if you can find an alternative by looking up at the clouds and the Sun, feeling the breeze on your face, or bringing fresh flowers into your home to enjoy.

Libras and Stress

Some Sun signs thrive on chaos and disorder, but not Libras. No, we spend a lot of time juggling the many different aspects of our lives in order to maintain balance, but occasionally, something has to give. We end up feeling imbalanced, off-kilter, and even downright cranky, all of which stress us out even more. So how do we avoid the stress triggers that we're naturally prone to?

Libras tend to get worked up by our sense of justice; if we think someone is being treated unfairly for no reason, you can bet we want to do something about it—but we also prefer to avoid conflict, so it can be a double-edged sword. We're naturally gifted communicators, so it's important to use our words like adults. If we see injustice and unfairness in the world, stewing over it while remaining silent will just frazzle us; it's often better to speak up in the moment, rather than spending weeks wishing we'd said something.

We also have a tendency to keep our problems to ourselves. Libras are great at listening to other people's problems, but we don't want to be a bother ... so we just act like everything is fine when inside, we're a complete dumpster fire. If you, like many Libras, spend a lot of time pretending you're okay when you're not, it's important to talk about your feelings, and that includes asking for professional help if you have to. All those friends who come to you when they need support will be there for you when you need support in turn—you won't be a bother at all. In fact, they'll probably be honored you chose them as a confidant in your time of need.

Additionally, Libras like to maintain harmony and balance in our relationships, and sometimes that manifests as too many commitments to too many people. Have you overscheduled yourself again? Do you agree to do things for everyone else, but fail to leave time for your own self-care? Try to avoid stretching yourself too thin. No one will be mad if you say no when you're overcommitted—*no* is a complete sentence. Don't worry about trying to be a people pleaser; instead, just be your authentic self. The people who matter in your life will love you for it and appreciate you just the way you are.

Building Altars of Self-Care

Angela Raincatcher

As a Libra witch, I seek to understand the world through connecting with others. Being in relationship with other beings—whether human, animals, or plant beings—I learn about the natural world, the gods, and myself. But sometimes I can get lost in my relationships and in my own head. When this happens, I find that my mind becomes a whirlwind of overlapping voices shouting conflicting ideas. I am frozen and cannot act. I become depressed and weighted down in despair. Not a good place for a Libra—much less anyone else.

Luckily, I have a practice that brings me out of the whirlwind of despair, helps me gain focus and peace, and appeals to my Libran creative sensibilities—and that is building an altar. This practice has no rules, and you do not need a witch's cabinet full of supplies. An altar doesn't have to be an elaborate production. Just by bringing together a few objects with intent and placing them in a way that is beautiful to your eye, you can create an altar of self-care. Let me show you through an example.

Recently my father-in-law died. Grieving his death also brought up guilt and grief from my own father's death over twenty years ago. At work I realized I had spent the whole day staring at my computer screen crying. I couldn't think. I couldn't write. And I had a deadline! So, when I got home, I went for a walk—just around my front yard. I gathered dark brown pine cones, yellow leaves, bright red berries, and green fir needles, and I placed them in my harvesting basket. Then I sat on the damp earth and began to breathe and ground. I sent my attention and energy down to connect with the life in the soil. I listened to my breath, to the wind, and to the birds. I found that inner core of peace that lives at the deep center of each of us—and I pulled that out into my hands. I let that energy guide me to pick up and place the cones, leaves, and berries into a mandala on the ground in front of me.

By finding and creating balance with the materials in my basket, I found and created balance within myself. I was able to pour my love for my father and my father-in-law into this offering—a small altar of beauty and love. I sat with my altar for a few minutes and just breathed, allowing the power of the natural world and the love of my beloved dead to work their magic on me and help me find my center.

But what if you are not at home or don't have anything at hand? You can still create an altar with pen and paper. I use simple icons to represent things I would place on my altar and perhaps craft a sigil for intent. Then I draw a circle around the whole thing to tie them together. It doesn't have to be perfect or fancy or understandable to anyone but you.

We Libra witches seek balance, beauty, and relationship in the world, and in our magic. Creating altars harnesses our inherent creativity and our desire to make the world a bit more beautiful—all while strengthening our connection and relationship with ourselves and the magical world around us.

DON'T BLAME IT
ON YOUR SUN SIGN

Patti Wigington

Even though we love to think we're always delightful and enchanting, we Libras sometimes fall into traps related to our Sun sign—because despite all our positive traits, we can also be prone to a few negative ones. It's important for us to recognize those personal pitfalls—not because we want to rant about them or make excuses, but because we can use these experiences to grow and develop. The typical Libra learns from their past mistakes because we really prefer to avoid repeating them.

Libras are charming, diplomatic, tactful souls. We dislike violence, injustice, and unfairness, and will take a stand, coolly and calmly, against any of those things when we witness them; even just *hearing* about them can fill us with outrage and righteous indignation. We're strongly opinionated but make an extra effort to be kind (or at least courteous) in our delivery. We need constant mental stimuli, as well as intellectual conversation and exposure to the arts and creative endeavors; we suck at meaningless small talk or trivial chitchat about things that don't interest us. We enjoy the benefits of deep relationships and collaborative effort, but we're equally comfortable with our own solitude. These are all traits that can endear us well to others; a Libra can fit in smoothly by adapting to just about any social situation, which we manage to navigate like very polite chameleons.

On the other hand, because we're so often focused on the needs of others, we have a tendency to fall into some negative habits, to our own detriment. Libras often lose track of their own well-being; we can hold on to a grudge like it's nobody's business, and we've been known to shut down—or at least, mentally check out—when a situation isn't going in our favor. I'll be the first to admit I've been guilty of all these things over the years—and rather than see them as excuses for why I do the things I do, I've learned to understand my own warning signals so I can navigate around them when I start to see these behaviors looming on my horizon.

Neglecting Self-Care

I'm a fixer. I can't help it, it's just my nature—whether it's a Libra thing or because it's just the way my brain is wired, I'm all about finding solutions. I'm a problem-solver, both in my professional life in the corporate world, and in my interpersonal relationships. Sometimes it's a challenge for me to know whether other people really want solutions, or whether they just need support—and I've learned to ask which one it is. I can provide either, but I need some direction occasionally to make sure I'm on the right path.

Like most Libras, I spend a lot of time listening to the problems of other people and making sure everyone's needs are met. If we meet at a party, I'll be the one guaranteeing everyone is having a nice time and no one feels left out—I can work a room like you wouldn't believe. I'm the therapy friend, the one people open up to when things are going badly; if you're a Libra, you're probably that friend in the circle too.

Here's the problem—and it took me a long time to recognize it.

When we get so focused on fixing the problems of others that we neglect our own issues, when we're so busy trying to repair the broken world around us that we forget to fix the damage in our own lives, we get burned out. Our feelings get hurt, we feel emotionally injured, and holy cow, do we get resentful.

It's easy to blame this on "Well, I'm a Libra and that's how it is." But it's crucial for us to learn to prioritize our own needs—self-care isn't selfish. It's transformative and empowering, and effective self-care allows us to focus on our own pain, stress, anxiety, or emotional baggage. As we take the time to heal ourselves, it opens us up to helping others in a way that includes healthy boundaries.

When my children were younger, everything I did revolved around making sure their world was a good one. I volunteered in the community, I helped out in their schools, I arranged my work schedule around the times I needed to be Mom's Taxi Service. And after a dozen or so years of that, I realized I'd lost myself a bit. I didn't have anything at all that was just about *me*, it was all about my family, and it made me sad that my entire identity was wrapped up in being a parent. Don't get me wrong, my kids are awesome—but I was teaching them that I, as an adult, had no agency of my own because everything I did was focused on them.

So, I started treating myself to small acts of Me Time. I'd go out for dinner with a group of girlfriends on a Friday evening, letting my kids know they needed to arrange their own transportation to and from the high school football game (plot twist: literally all they had to do was ask their dad). I learned that it was okay to say no when I was asked to chair yet another PTO committee; turns out nobody got mad at me for turning down the work, they just went on and called the next volunteer on the list. After a decade and a half of cutting my own hair with a pair of sewing scissors, I allowed myself to go see a professional stylist and bask in the luxury of someone else shampooing my head and giving me an amazing haircut (I still see that same stylist ten years later, and she's still a total rock star).

These may not sound like much, but for me, they were huge. I learned to find myself again in those moments of Me Time, and also allowed my kids to grow into self-sufficient adults with a healthy, well-adjusted mother.

Small actions = big results.

Carrying a Grudge

Libras are well known for being easygoing—we try to avoid conflict when possible, and we're tactful and kind to a degree that others might find downright obnoxious. So how can Libras at the same time be grudge holders?

We value relationships and connection, so if someone does us wrong, we'll do our best to work things out. We'll compromise, negotiate, listen to the other person's side of the story—a Libra will basically serve as a self-mediator in any case of disagreement. We're willing to do the work as necessary, until everyone is happy again. But remember that whole thing about how much we value trust and fairness? If someone breaks our trust or exhibits signs that they are unkind or disloyal, then watch out. Because we will nurse that for a *really* long time. We like to believe we can forgive and forget…but Libras never forget. And if the transgression is big enough, we'll rarely let that person back into our lives.

When I was in my late thirties, I made a new friend. We bumped into each other where I worked, struck up a conversation, and hit it off swimmingly. Obviously, it's nice to have a new friend—especially as an adult, when it's often hard to meet people—so we hung out a few times, getting to know each other and discovering we had a lot in common. But as I got to know her better, I started to notice some things she said in passing that made my Spidey senses tingle, and I began to wonder if she wasn't quite the person I thought she was. There were very small red flags at first, and I tried asking clarifying questions to make sure I wasn't misunderstanding her intent—after all, Libras generally try to see the best in everyone.

And then she made a vicious, hateful statement about a particular group of people—a group of which I am part, as are several people I care about deeply. I was horrified. How could I have been fooled into thinking she was a good person, when she had opinions like that? I did my due diligence, challenging her on it … and she simply doubled down and restated her opinions even more firmly. That was when I realized I couldn't trust her. I knew that I—and my friends and family—would not be safe around her. I made the conscious and deliberate decision to end the friendship then and there. Later, she reached out with some sort of noncommittal "I'm sorry you were offended blah blah blah" apology, but the damage was done. I could never be friends with this person again and had zero interest in any sort of interaction with her. She broke my trust, and once that's lost, there's no getting it back.

So how do we avoid holding grudges against people who hurt us? My key takeaway from this experience was the importance of watching for those red flags from the beginning. I saw a few telltale signs right off the bat that things weren't what they seemed but ignored them because I was too busy trying to give her the benefit of the doubt. If I'd paid attention to her toxic behavior and recognized it from the start, I'd never have been friends with her in the first place. And then I wouldn't have had to cut her out of my life and go through the drama of ending the friendship.

I learned that for me, boundaries sometimes have to be more than just lines in the sand—they may need to be deal-breakers.

Shutting It All Down

Libras thrive on social interaction and personal connection—we need others as much as they need us—but sometimes, it's all a bit much. It's easy for us to fall into the trap of checking out of a situation when we get overwhelmed. The problem that arises here is that if we shut down mentally and emotionally, we sometimes leave other people confused and wondering what the heck happened.

I've found that in my interpersonal relationships, it's important for me to be mindful of how I'm communicating with the other person. In particular, I've had dealings with people in my life that made me feel like I was speaking to a potted plant, for all the reaction I got from them. Find your needs unmet and your words dismissed often enough, and it's pretty easy to just stop sharing how you feel. After all, why bother, right? The other person isn't going to listen. And Libras *hate* feeling like they're not being listened to, because we do value connection so much.

If I'm upset or angry about something, I can stew on it for a while (oh, hey, what a surprise, all of the Libra pitfalls are interconnected!) before I actually try to clear the air. But what's far worse is when I *never* try to clear the air, I just stop caring and go silent. I've learned that it's important for me to make it clear that I'm about to check out. I've used phrases like *If you don't start acknowledging my concerns, I'm going to stop sharing them with you* or *When I feel like I'm being ignored, it makes me less likely to speak about how I feel.* While I don't go as far as issuing ultimatums—it's not really my style—I do know that it's crucial for me to use my words like a grown-up, and let the other person know we're on precarious ground. If I don't, then I feel I have to take partial responsibility when I shut down completely.

Being an angry Libra is frustrating enough—but it feels even worse to be an indifferent, disengaged one.

Rose Ritual to
Balance and Boost Libra Power

By Astrea Taylor

From time to time, Libras need to rebalance and recharge their energy. This ritual bestows equilibrium and reminds you of your inherent power. Roses are used in this ritual due to their association with Venus, Libra's ruling planet, and because their aroma is said to bestow supreme relaxation. If you can't find a thornless rose, cut off the thorns with a knife so you can enter a trance state without worrying about being pricked. If you don't have a rose, you can use any other flower or herb as long as it empowers you, it's nontoxic, and you're not allergic. The best time for this ritual is after a shower or a bath so you'll have a clean slate, energetically. The use of a wall mirror is optional; use it only if it's beneficial.

You will need:

+ A thornless rose
+ A small bowl of water (if possible, use spring water or purified water)
+ A wall mirror (optional)

Stand before the mirror, undressed or dressed to your level of comfort. Take a moment to notice the beauty of the rose. Appreciate its color, shape, and delicate petals. Breathe deeply and inhale the aroma, if there is one. Speak the intention aloud:

Libra powers, arise within me—
charisma, balance, art, intelligence, and beauty.

Dip the rose into the bowl of water and gently shake off the excess. Gaze at your reflection in the mirror with soft, kind eyes. Begin to caress your face with the wet rose, using slow and deliberate movements. Take pleasure in the feeling of the smooth petals gliding across your cheeks, forehead, and chin. Lose yourself in the sensations.

When you've caressed your entire face, dip the flower into the water and recite the intention again. Use the rose to delicately caress your neck and collarbone. Take as much time as you need to savor the feelings that come up and enter an entranced state of mind. Repeat the steps with your chest, arms, hands, torso, back, legs, and feet, until the rose has touched every part of the body you wish to caress.

When you're done, take a few deep, satisfying breaths. With every inhalation, feel your Libra powers increase— breathe in the power of charisma, balance, art, intelligence, and beauty. When you feel yourself brimming with this energy, give yourself a hug to seal the magic in.

Place the flower in a vase to remind you of your inner fortitude over the next few days. You can either let your skin air-dry, or you can towel off. Get dressed, knowing that your Libra powers are intact and ready for whatever the day may bring!

POSTCARD FROM A LIBRA WITCH

Both Sides Now: Overcoming Psychic Indecision

Tomás Prower

The judges of the zodiac. Wisdom and the seemingly preternat-ural ability to see through subjectivity and weigh facts against "facts." But when we have to point that perception at ourselves, gaze inward to decipher the truth among the "truths" as we would like them to be about ourselves, we falter and misjudge, convinc-ing ourselves that our wants, our needs, our desires, are objective truths, when really, they're subjective "truths."

So then, how does the scale measure itself? Well...it can't. It needs another apparatus to help, and in terms of magic, the apparatus I use is a simple enchanted coin because it can be used anywhere at any time very inconspicuously. All you need is any coin and your own mind.

One personal instance, in particular, wherein this bit of enchantment helped me was when I was lost in love. I was enam-ored over this guy I had been dating, but the romance (which we Libras do love) had fizzled out. I wasn't getting my emotional needs met, but I still cared deeply for this guy, as he cared for me. Should I stay or should I go? It was time to consult the coin.

First, I got into a meditational state and evoked the pow-ers of deities and historical figures whose guidance and wisdom I trusted and admired (though ancestors, fictional characters, and the abstract Tao work, too), asking that they impart their objective wisdom into the coin so as to overcome the psychic subjectiveness with which "love" often blinds us.

Then I thanked those who participated in the magic as I sat in contemplation of the coin, being open to any parting wisdom from all those I called upon for aid. And that's it; the spell work was complete.

Next it was time for the action part. I placed the coin on my thumb and flipped it into the air. Heads, I stay and try to reignite the flames of passion; tails, I leave into single-ness and search for someone more fulfilling. As it descended, I caught it and covered the result. At that moment, the magic kicked in. Deep in my gut, I had a flash of "I really hope it isn't heads so that I don't have to keep trying to make this work." And there's my answer from the divine. The actual result of the coin flip was (and always is with this spell) irrelevant. The enchanted answer was the one that penetrated my subjec-tiveness in that undeniable split-second before the reveal, and I knew it was the answer because it had me "hoping" for the result I was always dreading before the spell.

Try it sometime and become a better judge over yourself and your own mind. As for me, the search for love continues, but I sure as hell have had major upgrades in romance since leaving that guy who didn't make me feel like magic!

SPIRIT OF LIBRA GUIDANCE RITUAL

Ivo Dominguez, Jr.

The signs are more than useful constructs in astrology or categories for describing temperaments; they are also powerful and complicated spiritual entities. So, what is meant when we say a sign is a spirit? I often describe the signs of the zodiac as the twelve forms of human wisdom and folly. The signs are twelve styles of human consciousness, which also means the signs are well-developed group minds and egregores. Think on the myriad of people over thousands of years who have poured energy into the constructs of the signs through intentional visualization and study. Moreover, the lived experience of each person as one of the signs is deposited into the group minds and egregores of their sign. Every Libra who has ever lived or is living contributes to the spirit of Libra.

The signs have a composite nature that allows them to exist in many forms on multiple planes of reality at once. In addition to the human contribution to their existence, the spirits of the signs are made from inputs from all living beings in our world, whether they are made of dense matter or of spiritual substances. These vast and ancient thoughtforms that became group minds and then egregores are also vessels that can be used by divine beings to communicate with humans. The spirits of the signs can manifest themselves as small as a sprite or larger than the Earth. The shape and the magnitude of the spirit of Libra emerging before you will depend on who you are and how and why you call upon them.

There are many good ways to be a witch and a multitude of well-developed approaches to performing rituals. The ritual described in this chapter may or may not match your accustomed style, but for your first attempt, I encourage you to try it as it is written. Once you've experienced it, then you'll see which parts, if any, you wish to adjust to be a better fit for you. I'll give some suggestions on how to do so at the end of this chapter.

Purpose and Use

This ritual will make it possible to commune with the spirit of Libra. The form the spirit will take will be different each time you perform the ritual. What appears will be determined by what you are looking for and your state of mind and soul. The process for preparing yourself for the ritual will do you good as well. Aligning yourself with the source and core of your energy is a useful practice in and of itself. Exploring your circumstances, motivations, and intentions is a valuable experience whether or not you are performing this ritual.

If you have a practical problem you are trying to solve or an obstacle that must be overcome, the spirit of Libra may have useful advice. If you are trying to better understand who you are and what you are striving to accomplish, then the spirit of Libra can be your mentor. Should you have a need to recharge yourself or flush out stale energy, you can use this ritual to reconnect with a strong clear current of power that is compatible with your core. This energy can be used for magickal empowerment, physical vitality, or healing, or redirected for spell work. If you are charging objects or magickal implements with Libra energy, this ritual can be used for this purpose as well.

Timing for the Ritual

The prevailing astrological conditions have an impact on how you experience a ritual, the type and amount of power available, and the outcomes of the work. If you decide you want to go deeper in your studies of astrology, you'll find many simple or elaborate techniques to either pick the best day and time or to adjust your ritual to work with what fits your schedule. Thankfully, the ritual to meet the spirit of your sign does not require exact timing or perfect astrological conditions. This ritual depends on your inner connection to your Sun sign, so it is not as reliant on the external celestial conditions as some other rituals. Each of us has worlds within ourselves, which include inner landscapes and inner skies. Your birth chart, and the sky that it depicts, burns brightest within you. Although not required, you can improve the effectiveness of this ritual if you use any of the following simple guidelines for favorable times:

+ When the Moon or the Sun is in Libra.
+ When Venus is in Libra.
+ On Friday, the day of Venus, and even better at dawn.

+ At sunset when the Sun on the horizon forms the glyph of Libra.

Materials and Setup

The following is a description of the physical objects that will make it easier to perform this ritual. Don't worry if you don't have all of them as, in a pinch, you need no props. However, the physical objects will help anchor the energy and your mental focus.

You will need:

+ A printout of your birth chart
+ A table to serve as an altar
+ A chair if you want to sit during the ritual
+ A small dish or tray with flower petals to represent the element of air
+ An assortment of items for the altar that correspond to Libra or Venus (for example, a citrine, a carrot or lemon, and lavender flowers)
+ A pad and a pen or chalk and a small blackboard, or something else you can use to draw a glyph

Before beginning the ritual, you may wish to copy the ritual invocations onto paper or bookmark this chapter and bring the book into the ritual. I find that the process of writing out the invocation, whether handwritten or typed, helps forge a better connection with the words and their meaning. If possible, put the altar table in the center of your space, and if not, then as close to due east as you can manage. Place the dish with petals on the altar and hold your hand over it. Send sparks of energy from your hand to the petals. Put the printout of your birth chart on the altar to one side of the petals and arrange the items you have selected to anchor the Libra and Venus energy around them. To the other side of the petals, place the pad and pen. Make sure you turn off your phone, close the door, close the curtains, or do whatever else is needed to prevent distractions.

Ritual to Meet the Spirit of Your Sign

You may stand or be seated; whichever is the most comfortable for you. Begin by focusing on your breathing. When you pay attention to the process of breathing, you become more aware of your body, the flow of your life energy, and the balance between conscious and unconscious actions. After you have done so for about a minute, it is time to shift into fourfold breathing. This consists of four phases: inhaling, lungs full, exhaling, and lungs empty. You count to keep time so that each of the four phases is of equal duration. Try a count of four or five in your first efforts. Depending on your lungs and how fast you count, you will need to adjust the number higher or lower. When you hold your breath, hold it with your belly muscles, not your throat. When you hold your breath in fourfold breathing, your throat should feel relaxed. Be gentle and careful with yourself if you have asthma, high blood pressure, are late in pregnancy, or have any other condition that may have an impact on your breathing and blood pressure. In general, if there are difficulties, they arise during the lungs' full or empty phases because of holding them by clenching the throat or compressing the lungs. The empty and the full lungs should be held by the position of the diaphragm, and the air passages left open. After one to three minutes of fourfold breathing, you can return to your normal breathing pattern.

Now, close your eyes and move your center of consciousness down into the middle of your chest. Proceed with grounding and centering, dropping and opening, shifting into the alpha state, or whatever practice you use to reach the state of mind that supports ritual work. Then gaze deeply inside yourself and find yourself sitting on the ground in a garden. Look at the beauty of the crystal and the plant materials. Take a breath and smell fresh air and refreshing fragrances. Pick up a petal and gently move the air with it and awaken all the places and spaces within you that are of Libra. When you feel ready, open your eyes.

Zodiac Casting

If you are seated, stand if you are able and face the east. Slowly read this invocation aloud, putting some energy into your words. As you read, slowly turn counterclockwise so that you come full circle when you reach the last line. Another option is to hold your hand over your head and trace the counterclockwise circle of the zodiac with your finger.

> *I call forth the twelve to join me in this rite.*
> *I call forth Aries and the power of courage.*
> *I call forth Taurus and the power of stability.*
> *I call forth Gemini and the power of versatility.*
> *I call forth Cancer and the power of protection.*
> *I call forth Leo and the power of the will.*
> *I call forth Virgo and the power of discernment.*
> *I call forth Libra and the power of harmony.*
> *I call forth Scorpio and the power of renewal.*
> *I call forth Sagittarius and the power of vision.*
> *I call forth Capricorn and the power of responsibility.*
> *I call forth Aquarius and the power of innovation.*
> *I call forth Pisces and the power of compassion.*
> *The power of the twelve is here.*
> *Blessed be!*

Take a few deep breaths and shift your gaze to each of the items on the altar. Become aware of the changes in the atmosphere around you and the presence of the twelve signs.

Altar Work

Pick up the printout of your birth chart and look at your chart. Touch each of the twelve houses with your finger and push energy into them. You are energizing and awakening your birth chart to act as a focal point of power on the altar. Put your chart back on the altar when it feels ready to you. Then take the pad and pen and write the glyph for Libra again and again. The glyphs can be different sizes, they can overlap; you can make any pattern with them you like so long as you pour energy into the ink as you write. Scribing the glyph is an action that helps draw the interest of the spirit of Libra. Periodically look at the items on the altar as you continue scribing the glyph. When you feel sensations in your body, such as electric tingles, warmth, shivers, or something that you associate with the approach of a spirit, it is time to move on to the next step. If these are new experiences for you, just follow your instincts. Put away the pen and paper and pick up the sheet with the invocation of Libra.

Invoking Libra

Before beginning to read this invocation, get in touch with your feelings. Think on what you hope to accomplish in this ritual and why it matters to you. Then speak these lines slowly and with conviction.

> *Libra, hear me, for I am born of the wind's*
>   *cardinal air.*
> *Libra, see me, for the Libra Sun shines upon*
>   *me.*
> *Libra, know me as a member of your family*
>   *and your company.*
> *Libra, know me as your student and your*
>   *protégé.*
> *Libra, know me as a conduit for your power.*
> *Libra, know me as a wielder of your magick.*
> *I am of you, and you are of me.*
> *I am of you, and you are of me.*
> *I am of you, and you are of me.*
> *Libra is here within and without.*
> *Blessed be!*

Your Requests

Close your eyes and look within for several deep breaths, and silently or aloud welcome the spirit of Libra. Close your eyes and ask for any guidance that would be beneficial for you and listen. It may take some time before anything comes through, so be patient. I find it valuable to receive guidance before making a request so that I can refine or modify intentions and outcomes. Consider the meaning of whatever impressions or guidance you received and reaffirm your intentions and desired outcomes for this ritual.

It is more effective to use multiple modes of communication to make your request. Speak silently or aloud the words that describe your need and how it could be solved. Visualize the same message but without the words and project the images on your mind's screen. Then put all your attention on your feelings and your bodily sensations that have been stirred up by contemplating your appeal to the spirit of Libra. Once again wait and use all your physical and psychic senses to perceive what is given. At this point in the ritual, if there are objects to be charged, touch them or focus your gaze on them.

Offer Gratitude

You may be certain or uncertain about the success of the ritual or the time frame for the outcomes to become clear. Regardless of that, it is a good practice to offer thanks and gratitude to the spirit of Libra for being present. Also, thank yourself for doing your part of the work. The state of heart and mind that comes with thanks and gratitude makes it easier for the work to become manifest. Thanks and gratitude also act as a buffer against the unintended consequences that can be put into motion by rituals.

Release the Ritual

If you are seated, stand if you are able and face the east. Slowly turn clockwise until you come full circle while repeating the following or something similar.

> *Return, return oh turning wheel to your*
> *starry home.*
> *Farewell, farewell oh gracious Libra until we*
> *speak again.*

Another option while saying these words is to hold your hand over your head and trace a clockwise circle of the zodiac with your finger. When you are done, look at your chart on the altar and say,

It is done. It is done. It is done.

Afterward

I encourage you to write down your thoughts and observations of what you experienced in the ritual. Do this while it is still fresh in mind before the details begin to blur. The information will become more useful over time as you work more with the spirit of Libra. It will also let you evaluate the outcomes of your workings and improve your process in future workings. This note-taking or journaling will also help you dial in any changes or refinements to this ritual for future use. Contingent upon the guidance you received or the outcomes you desire, you may want to add reminders to your calendar.

More Options

These are some modifications to this ritual you may wish to try:

+ Put together or purchase Libra incense to burn during the ritual. A Libra oil to anoint the petals or yourself is another possibility.

+ Set up a richer and deeper altar. In addition to adding more objects that resonate to the energy of Libra or Venus, consecrate each object before the ritual. You may also want to place an altar cloth on the table that brings to mind Libra, Venus, or the element of air.

+ Creating a sigil to concentrate the essence of what you are working toward would be a good addition to the altar.

+ Consider adding chanting, free-form toning, or movement to raise energy for the altar work and/or for invoking Libra.

+ If you feel inspired, you can write your own invocations for calling the zodiac and/or invoking Libra. This is a great way to deepen your understanding of the signs and to personalize your ritual.

Rituals have greater personal meaning and effectiveness when you personalize them and make them your own.

LIBRA ANOINTING OIL RECIPE

* * *

Ivo Dominguez, Jr.

This oil is used for charging and consecrating candles, crystals, and other objects you use in your practice. This oil makes it easier for an object to be imbued with Libra energy. It also primes and tunes the objects so your will and power as a Libra witch flow more easily into them. Do not apply the oil to your skin unless you have done an allergy test first.

Ingredients:

+ Carrier oil—1 ounce
+ Ylang-ylang—6 drops
+ Lavender—5 drops
+ Spruce—4 drops
+ Nutmeg—4 drops
+ Violet leaf—2 drops

Pour one ounce of a carrier oil into a small bottle or vial. The preferred carrier oils are almond oil or fractionated coconut oil. Other carrier oils can be used. If you use olive oil, the blend will have a shorter shelf life. Ideally use essential oils, but fragrance oils can be used as substitutes. Add the drops of the essential oils into the carrier. Once they are all added, cap the bottle tightly, and shake the bottle several times. Hold the bottle in your hands, take a breath, and pour energy into the oil. Visualize light pink or lavender energy or repeat the word *Libra* or raise energy in your preferred manner. Continue doing so until the oil feels warm, seems to glow, or you sense it is charged.

Label the bottle and store the oil in a cool, dark place. Consider keeping a little bit of each previous batch of oil to add to the new batch. This helps build the strength and continuity of the energy and intentions you have placed in the oil. Over time, that link makes your oils more powerful.

• BETTER EVERY DAY: THE WAY FORWARD •

Patti Wigington

L ook, we don't choose our Sun sign, it chooses us. There's nothing we can do to change it, whether we like it or not. So why not embrace it? If you take these simple actions to celebrate your Libra energy and live each day as if it's the best one ever, then it will be.

Libra Witchcraft on the Daily

Use your natural creative skills to make magic. Libras love beauty in all its many forms, so why not take advantage of it? Find ways to incorporate painting, writing, dance, music, or other skills into your rituals and spells. Sketch a picture of your magical intention, compose a song or chant to honor the divine, choreograph an interpretive dance to celebrate your own place in our universe. Do you keep a book of shadows or spell book? Make it aesthetically appealing by adding drawings, colorful artwork, or a collage of images that represent your Libra witch magic.

Incorporate self-care into your spiritual practice. You can make magic *and* take care of yourself at the same time. Remember those luxurious baths we talked about? Why not use those as a way of cleansing yourself metaphysically, using them in banishing magic, or crafting a relaxing meditation around your tub time? Do you like to smell pretty? Work with essential oil blends based on magical purposes—you'll smell fantastic and manifest your intentions at the same time. Learn to work with self-care practices that can help you realign any off-kilter energy, bring balance and harmony to your life, and ultimately help you connect to your higher self—try yoga, journaling, and meditation. Get into the habit of cleansing your physical and spiritual spaces, eliminating negative energy to make room for the positive and help inspire inner peace.

Carry healing, grounding crystals and other talismans with you that resonate with Libra vibrations. Lapis can help with decision-making because it helps support our truth—both hearing and speaking it. Citrine is a great stone to have on hand when you're meeting people for the first time; although Libras are naturally social, a piece of citrine can help us make a really positive and cheerful first impression. Black tourmaline helps keep us spiritually and emotionally grounded and balanced, especially when we know we're about to deal with conflict. Think about using a piece of green aventurine to invite good luck and abundance into your life—it will help you view different points of view objectively and open up new opportunities.

Take advantage of the Libra's innate connection to nature. Take a hike and hug a tree so you can connect to the Earth's energy, lie in the grass for quiet meditation, or go wildcrafting for herbs and other plants in the wild. If you've got space for a garden—whether it's in a big backyard or in containers on your windowsill—spending time with plants and soil can help you stabilize and become more grounded. Decorate your home with found items from the natural world. Vases of flowers and herbs, boughs of greenery, interesting bits of wood, bowls of pretty stones or seashells—you name it, a Libra can find a way to make it attractive! Don't forget about the magic of air energy as well—on days when it's pleasant outside, open windows and doors, and let the fresh breeze blow through your space. You'll feel revitalized and rejuvenated, and you'll have the added benefit of welcoming the air element into your home for magical activities.

Go with your gut! As a Libra, you're naturally intuitive—learn to trust your instinct. Try doing things without waiting for input and suggestions from others. Learning to rely on your intuition is a great trait for Libra witches—it gives us a definite advantage in regard to divination and other psychic abilities. If you've never tried divination, now is a good time to start practicing and seeing what methods you connect to best. Pick up a deck of tarot cards, runes, or a pendulum; try scrying with mirrors, crystals, or a bowl of water; or even make up a method that's unique to your own background and skill set.

Candle Ritual for Decision-Making

A struggle with decision-making can be an issue for Libras—but we're not indecisive most of the time. Instead, we like to restore balance to a situation and listen to different points of view. Libras are pretty flexible and are comfortable with changing our minds when presented with new information before making a decision. This candle ritual can help you make the best choice when you find yourself over-analyzing a situation.

You will need:
+ A white candle
+ Pen and paper

Make sure you have some time set aside for this ritual, where you won't be interrupted. Begin by sitting comfortably and taking a few deep breaths. Allow yourself to relax and let go of any stress or tension that you may be holding. Light a white candle and place it in front of you. Visualize the flame as a symbol of your inner wisdom and intuition. Take a piece of paper and a pen and write down the strengths and weaknesses of each option. Be honest and authentic as you consider each option.

As you write, take breaks to close your eyes and connect with your intuition. Focus on your breath and allow yourself to tune in to your inner guidance. When you have finished, review your list. Reflect on the qualities that are most important to you and how each option aligns with your values.

Take a deep breath and ask for guidance from your higher self, your deities, or the universe. Trust in your ability to make a decision that aligns with your highest good. When you're ready, blow out the candle and put the paper aside. Take a few moments to sit quietly and reflect on your choice, and trust in your own ability to find the best path forward as you make decisions with a sense of balance and harmony.

Immerse Yourself in Libra Energy

Learn to find balance in all things. Take deliberate steps to cultivate harmony in your life, whether it's your personal relationships, your professional success, your spiritual outlook, or the state of your physical body. Finding balance isn't something that will happen overnight—at least not for most of us—but we can engage in a learning process that will help us reach those goals. We're on a nearly constant quest for peace and harmony, but it's a lifelong journey, not a sprint.

Libras are pretty confident in general, but we sometimes have to work at it to have a healthy sense of self-esteem. Start being mindful of your own abilities and weaknesses, accept them, and find ways to be the best you can. When you figure out your own strengths, highlight them so you can shine in any situation. Give yourself a few minutes a day—or more, if you need it—just to focus on yourself. Remind yourself of what you've done well that day, and what challenges you've faced (and the lessons learned from both).

Practice gratitude daily. Libras celebrate their Sun sign during a time of year when many people reflect on things for which they're thankful. The fall equinox is celebrated as the time of the second harvest in many witchcraft traditions, and it's a period of abundance, bounty, and blessings. Train yourself to find things to be appreciative of regularly, and you'll soon find that you're attracting even more to be thankful for.

Recognize your bonds with friends and family as sacred. Make time for meaningful relationships—and that includes finding a balance between giving and receiving, whether it's communication, love, or support. Libras tend to be very selective when it comes to interpersonal connections and usually value quality over quantity. Cultivate a circle of people who lift you up rather than pushing you down, and you'll be able to share life's joys and challenges together.

Being Your Best Libra Self

Being aware of your own shortcomings and evaluating the lessons they offer can aid any Libra in being proactive when it comes to dealing with your more challenging traits. You can see a glass as half empty, sure … but you'll live a happier, more productive life if you see it as half full. Why not see the positive? Turn some of your Libra struggles into Libra advantages by learning from them and enjoy the benefits of living the best life you can.

Watch out for your own sense of self-indulgence. Take some time to think things through before you commit, and you're less likely to experience remorse and regrets later. Be authentic. Allow your true colors to shine through when you interact with others and let them see you for who you really are. Don't waste time with people who look down their nose at your positive, balanced vibe, or who exhibit unfair, judgmental, or toxic behavior. Focus on the people and situations needing your attention in the present and show your appreciation for what you have rather than obsessing over what you don't. Wherever you are, be there.

Meditation for the Libra Witch to Stay Focused

A bored Libra can tap out of a situation pretty easily once we become indifferent, despite being one of the more emotionally invested Sun signs. Even when we have a tendency to react to other people with love and affection, once we decide we're not interested in investing our time and energy, it's very easy for us to lose focus. Becoming more self-aware can help you give space to things that need your attention and allow you to step away from the stuff that's not really important in the grand scheme of things. Try this simple calming meditation to help yourself regain focus in the areas of your life in which you need it the most.

Begin by finding a quiet and peaceful place where you can sit or lie down comfortably. Take a few deep breaths and allow your body and mind to relax. As a Libra, you value balance and harmony in your life—imagine yourself standing at the center of a scale. Visualize your doubts and distractions as weights on one side of the scale, and your goals and priorities on the other side.

As you breathe deeply, begin to let go of any issues that are weighing you down—the emotional, spiritual, and mental clutter that takes up too much space. Imagine each distraction as a balloon drifting away, or a cloud disappearing into the sky. As you release them, feel the weight on the scale shifting toward your goals and priorities. Allow yourself to feel a sense of clarity and focus as you become more grounded in the present moment.

Repeat the following affirmation to yourself. "I am focused and clear-minded. I trust my ability to stay on track and achieve my goals. Like the scales, I am balanced, steady, and harmonious in all I do." Repeat this mantra as many times as you need to and allow it to sink into your subconscious mind. You may even wish to write it down and keep it in a place of prominence as a regular reminder of where to shift your energies and attentions. When you feel ready, take a few more deep breaths and slowly open your eyes. Carry this sense of focus and clarity with you throughout your day, and trust in your ability to stay focused.

Your Sun sign is one of balance and harmony— embrace it and celebrate all the advantages it gives you! Cultivate your own intuition and learn to trust your inner guidance. Develop and maintain meaningful relationships with others. Avoid conflict when you can, but don't be afraid to stand up for your values and principles. Prioritize self-care, as this will help you maintain a sense of inner peace. By making a conscious effort to nurture balance and beauty in your life, you can create a beautiful, balanced, and magical life for yourself and those around you.

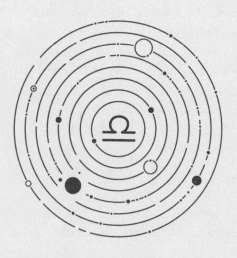

CONCLUSION

Ivo Dominguez, Jr.

no doubt, you are putting what you discovered in this book to use in your witchcraft. You may have a desire to learn more about how astrology and witchcraft fit together. One of the best ways to do this is to talk about it with other practitioners. Look for online discussions, and if there is a local metaphysical shop, check to see if they have classes or discussion groups. If you don't find what you need, consider creating a study group. Learning more about your own birth chart is also an excellent next step.

At some point, you may wish to call upon the services of an astrologer to give you a reading that is fine-tuned to your chart. There are services that provide not just charts but full chart readings that are generated by software. These are a decent tool and more economical than a professional astrologer, but they lack the finesse and intuition that only a person can offer. Nonetheless, they can be a good starting point. If you do decide to hire an astrologer to do your chart, shop around to find someone attuned to your spiritual needs. You may decide to learn enough astrology to read your own chart, and that will serve you for many reasons. However, for the same reasons that tarot readers will go to someone else for a reading, the same is true with astrological readers. It is hard to see some things when you are too attached to the outcomes.

If you find your interest in astrology and its effect on a person's relationship to witchcraft has been stimulated by this book, you may wish to read the other books in this series. Additionally, if you have other witches you work with, you'll find that knowing more about how they approach their craft will make your collective efforts more productive. Understanding them better will also help reduce conflicts or misunderstandings. The ending of this book is really the beginning of an adventure. Go for it.

LIBRA CORRESPONDENCES

September 22/23–October 22/23

Symbol: ♎

Solar System: Saturn, Venus

Season: Autumn

Day: Friday

Runes: Hagal, Tyr, Wyn

Element: Air

Colors: Black, Blue (Light), Royal Blue, Brown, Green, Lavender, Pink, Violet, Yellow

Energy: Yang

Chakras: Sacral, Heart

Number: 7

Tarot: Empress, Justice

Trees: Apple, Aspen, Cherry, Hazel, Magnolia, Maple, Witch Hazel

Herb and Garden: Catnip, Dandelion, Foxglove, Lilac, Marjoram, Mugwort, Passionflower, Pennyroyal, Rose, Spearmint, Strawberry, Thyme, Violet

Miscellaneous Plants: Aloe, Belladonna, Burdock, Mullein, Vanilla

Gemstones and Minerals: Agate, Ametrine, Aquamarine, Beryl, Bloodstone, Chrysoprase, Citrine, Desert Rose, Diamond, Emerald, Iolite, Jade, Jasper, Kunzite, Kyanite, Lapis Lazuli, Lepidolite, Malachite, Moonstone, Opal, Rose Quartz, Sapphire, Smoky Quartz, Sunstone, Tourmaline (Black, Blue, Pink), Zircon (Red)

Metals: Copper

From the Sea: Coral (Red)

Goddesses: Aphrodite, Athena, Frigg, Isis, Justitia, Maat, Minerva, Nemesis, Venus

Gods: Cernunnos, Hephaestus, Mithras, Njord, Shiva, Thoth, Vishnu

Angel: Raphael

Animals: Hare

Birds: Dove, Goose, Raven, Sparrow, Swan

Reptile: Snake

Issues, Intentions, and Powers: Attraction, Balance, Beauty, Business, Community, Cooperation, Fairness, Grace, Harmony, Justice, Love, Marriage, Relationships, Romance, Sensitivity, Sensuality, Sympathy, Unity

RESOURCES

Online

Astrodienst: Free birth charts and many resources.

+ https://www.astro.com/horoscope

Astrolabe: Free birth chart and software resources.

+ https://alabe.com

The Astrology Podcast: A weekly podcast hosted by professional astrologer Chris Brennan.

+ https://theastrologypodcast.com

Magazine

The world's most recognized astrology magazine (available in print and digital formats).

+ https://mountainastrologer.com

Books

+ *Practical Astrology for Witches and Pagans* by Ivo Dominguez, Jr.
+ *Parkers' Astrology: The Definitive Guide to Using Astrology in Every Aspect of Your Life* by Julia and Derek Parker

- *The Inner Sky: How to Make Wiser Choices for a More Fulfilling Life* by Steven Forrest
- *Predictive Astrology: Tools to Forecast Your Life and Create Your Brightest Future* by Bernadette Brady
- *Chart Interpretation Handbook: Guidelines for Understanding the Essentials of the Birth Chart* by Stephen Arroyo

CONTRIBUTORS

We give thanks and appreciation to all our guest authors who contributed their own special Libra energy to this project.

Dawn Aurora Hunt

Dawn Aurora Hunt, owner of Cucina Aurora Kitchen Witchery, is the author of *A Kitchen Witch's Guide to Love & Romance* and *Kitchen Witchcraft for Beginners*. Though not born under the sign of Libra, she combines knowledge of spiritual goals and magickal ingredients to create recipes for all Sun signs in this series. She is a Scorpio. Find her at www.CucinaAurora.com.

Emma Kathryn

Emma Kathryn, author of *Witch Life*, lives in Robin Hood County in the middle of England. Emma is a witch, vodouisant, and obeah woman practicing traditions that honor her heritage. When she's not reading, writing, or weaving magic, she can be found wandering the woods and wild places.

Kelden

Kelden is the author of *The Crooked Path: An Introduction to Traditional Witchcraft*, *The Witches' Sabbath: An Exploration of History, Folklore, and Modern Practice*, and *All Them Witches: Folktales & Rhymes*. Additionally, his writing has appeared in *The Witch's Altar*, *The New Aradia: A Witch's Handbook to Magical Resistance*, and *This Witch magazine*.

Sandra Kynes

Sandra Kynes (Midcoast Maine) is the author of seventeen books, including *Mixing Essential Oils for Magic*, *Magical Symbols and Alphabets*, *Crystal Magic*, *Plant Magic*, and *Sea Magic*. Excerpted content from her book *Llewellyn's Complete Book of Correspondences* has been used throughout this series, and she is a Scorpio. Find her at http://www.kynes.net.

Tomás Prower

Tomás Prower (he/him/él) is a graduate of UC: Santa Barbara who has worked for the French Government as a cultural liaison throughout South America, has been the External Relations Director for the Red Cross of Nevada, a mortician, and the author of books on multicultural magic. Website: www.tomasprower.com and www.instagram.com/tomasprower/.

Angela Raincatcher

Angela Raincatcher is a spirit-led visual artist, nature writer, and equal-opportunity polytheist living in Baltimore. She currently serves as Convener of Connect DC, which hosts public Pagan rituals celebrating the cycles of nature and life in Washington, DC. Follow her artwork, cats, gardening, and shenanigans on Instagram at @angela.raincatcher.

Astrea Taylor

Astrea Taylor is the author of *Intuitive Witchcraft*, *Modern Witchcraft with the Greek Gods*, *Air Magic*, and *Inspiring Creativity Through Magick*. In her books and classes, Astrea shares her love of science, magick, mental health, history, and energy awareness. Learn more at AstreaTaylor.com.

Manny Tejeda y Moreno

Manny Tejeda y Moreno is managing editor of *The Wild Hunt: Pagan News & Perspectives*. Born in Cuba and raised in the American South, Manny has been in the Pagan community for almost four decades, serving in different roles. He splits his time between South Florida and the Alban Hills.

Notes

Notes

Notes

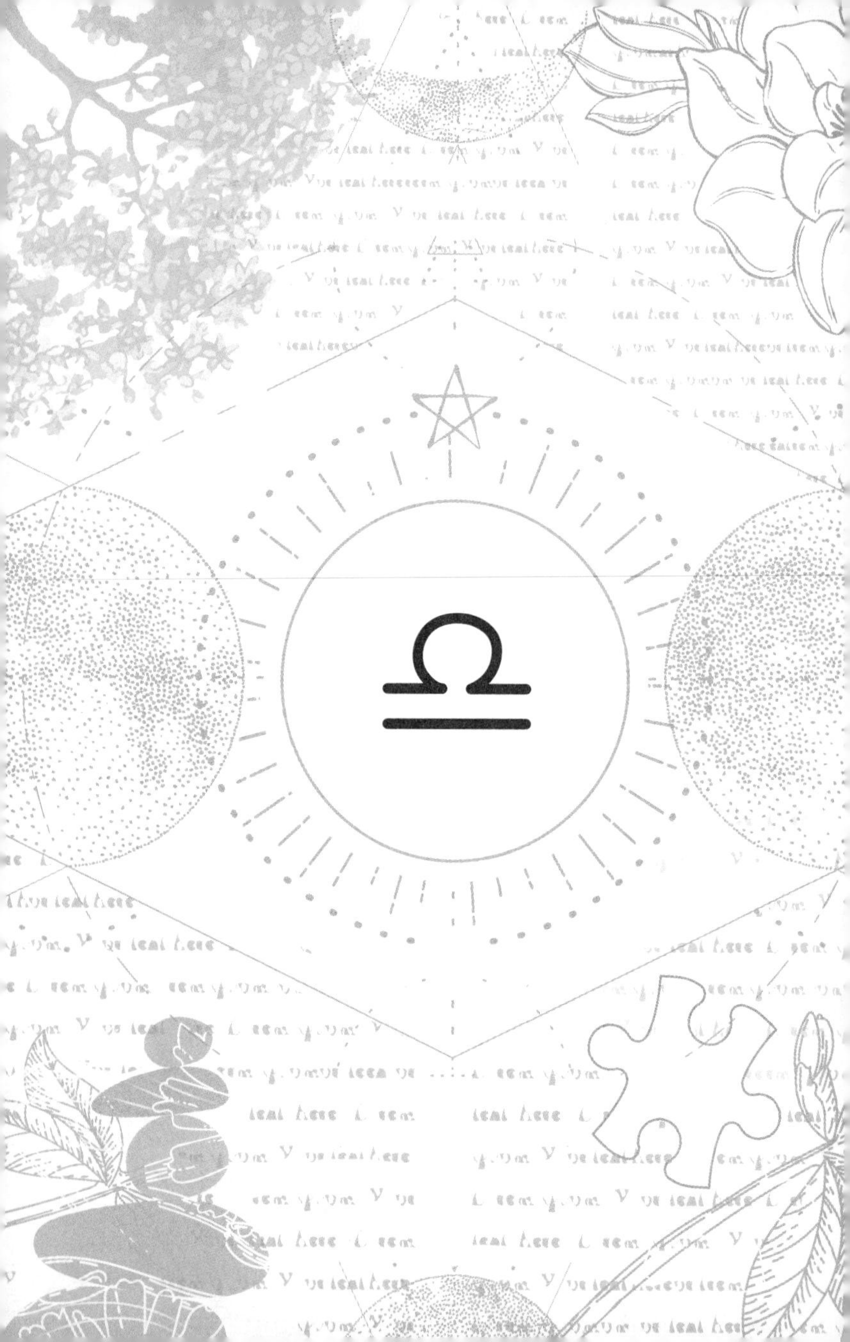

To Write to the Author

If you wish to contact the author or would like more information about this book, please write to the author in care of Llewellyn Worldwide Ltd. and we will forward your request. Both the author and the publisher appreciate hearing from you and learning of your enjoyment of this book and how it has helped you. Llewellyn Worldwide Ltd. cannot guarantee that every letter written to the author can be answered, but all will be forwarded. Please write to:

Ivo Dominguez, Jr.
Patti Wigington
℅ Llewellyn Worldwide
2143 Wooddale Drive
Woodbury, MN 55125-2989
Please enclose a self-addressed stamped envelope for reply,
or $1.00 to cover costs. If outside the U.S.A., enclose
an international postal reply coupon.

Many of Llewellyn's authors have websites with additional information and resources. For more information, please visit our website at:

www.llewellyn.com

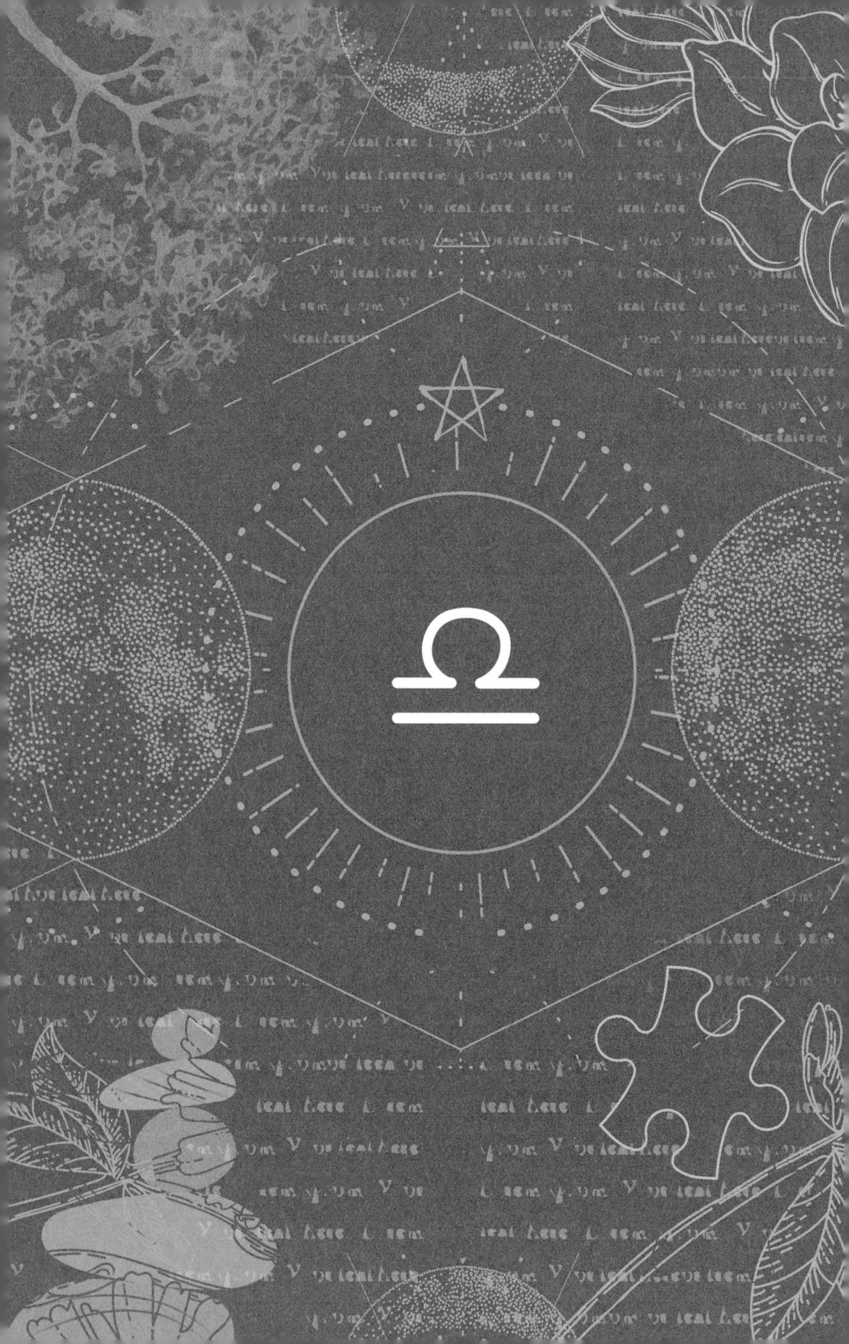